Welsh Nationalism
in the Twentieth Century

WELSH NATIONALISM IN THE TWENTIETH CENTURY

The Ethnic Option and the Modern State

Charlotte Aull Davies

PRAEGER

New York
Westport, Connecticut
London

Library of Congress Cataloging-in-Publication Data
Davies, Charlotte Aull.
  Welsh nationalism in the twentieth century : the ethnic option and the modern state / Charlotte Aull Davies.
    p. cm.
  Bibliography: p.
  Includes index.
  ISBN 0-275-93116-1 (alk. paper)
  1. Wales—Politics and government—20th century. 2. Nationalism—Wales—History—20th century. 3. Ethnology—Wales. I. Title.
DA722.D28 1989
942.9'0858—dc19   88-28832

Copyright © 1989 by Charlotte Aull Davies

All rights reserved. No portion of this book may be reproduced, by any process or technique, without the express written consent of the publisher.

Library of Congress Catalog Card Number: 88-28832
ISBN: 0-275-93116-1

First published in 1989

Praeger Publishers, One Madison Avenue, New York, NY 10010
A division of Greenwood Press, Inc.

Printed in the United States of America

The paper used in this book complies with the Permanent Paper Standard issued by the National Information Standards Organization (Z39.48–1984).

10 9 8 7 6 5 4 3 2 1

To all those in Wales
who helped to make this work possible —
Diolch o galon

Contents

Figures and Tables ix
Preface xi

1. Theoretical and Historical Background 1
   Ethnic Nationalism: Theoretical Perspective 2
   Ethnic Nationalism in Britain 8
   Welsh Nationalism: Nineteenth-Century Roots 10
   Welsh Nationalism: The Twentieth Century 14
   Summary 19

2. Nationalist Uses of the Past 21
   Welsh History: Alternative Interpretations 25
   National History and Nationalist Politics 29

3. Two Tongues, One Voice 37
   The Welsh Language and Plaid Cymru 41
   The Politicization of the Language Issue 45
   The Growth of a Language-based Infrastructure 51
   Summary 56

4. Toward a Welsh Economy 59
   Economic History of an Internal Colony 60
   Nationalist Response 65
   Summary 79

5. Rise and Decline with the Welfare State — 83
    The Welfare State and Community Institutions — 85
    The Welsh Office — 86
    The Wales Trades Union Council — 88
    Political Devolution and a Welsh Assembly — 91
    The Welsh Water Authority — 94
    The Welsh Infrastructure and the EEC — 97
    Summary — 98

6. Conclusions, Comparisons, and Forecasts — 101
    Structural Stimulants — 101
    Nationalist Groups — 105
    Some Comparisons — 108
    The Future — 111

Appendixes — 115
References — 123
Index — 133

Figures and Tables

Figure 1.1. Plaid Cymru Electoral History, General Elections 1945–1987   9

Figure 3.1. Distribution of the Welsh Language in 1971, by County   38

Table 3.1. Welsh Speakers in Wales, 1901–1981   39

Table 3.2. Organizations in the Welsh-language Infrastructure   55

Preface

The Welsh nationalist movement is representative of many ethnically based political separatist movements associated with the minority nationalities to be found in most European states. The majority of these movements can point to predecessors in the nineteenth century. However, the vigorous reemergence of minority nationalism in the second half of the twentieth century surprised academic and political establishments alike, and, as a result, ethnic nationalism has been a focus of scholarly debate for over two decades.

While this study does consider nineteenth-century antecedents, its emphasis is on Welsh nationalism since World War II. In strictly political terms, the major successes of the Welsh nationalist movement occurred in the late 1960s and early 1970s; since 1979, the movement has experienced a decline in electoral popularity, though gaining a third Member of Parliament in the 1987 general election. However, in the area of cultural nationalism, and particularly with regard to the Welsh language movement, Welsh nationalism has continued to display great vitality and to achieve significant advances. In consequence, the Welsh language is by far the most vigorous of the Celtic languages, whether measured in terms of official recognition, access to the mass media, use in education, or literary output.

Early theoretical explanations of ethnic nationalism were of a highly structural nature; in more recent years emphasis has been on individualistic explanations based on the theory of collective action. This study combines these levels of analysis by showing how specific structural factors (not general structural conditions) affected the decision-making processes of various categories of individuals to produce nationalist activists and voters. It also differs from many studies of ethnic nationalism in its treatment of the cultural bases of the movement. Rather than taking cultural distinctions to be primarily functional markers of identity, it details the substantive contributions of Welsh national history and the Welsh language to the movement.

Most of the formal data collection for this study was undertaken during three periods of research in Wales: a preliminary month's research in June 1975; one year's doctoral research between June 1976 and June 1977; and one year's postdoctoral research between September 1978 and August 1979. In addition, the author was continuously resident in Wales from 1979 to 1985, allowing for updating and additions to the main body of data. The principal research techniques employed were participant-observation and formal interviews. Participant-observation entailed intensive involvement in the Welsh nationalist movement in both its political and cultural manifestations. Formal interviews were conducted with Plaid Cymru national leaders and officers, Members of Parliament, prospective parliamentary candidates, local activists in both north and south Wales, older party members who could supply historical background, leaders and activists on both sides in the 1979 campaign preceding the Referendum on an Assembly for Wales, and representatives of most major Welsh organizations, both those comprising the Welsh bureaucracy and those representing various special interests. Data acquired by these means were supplemented by data from documentary sources and historical materials.

I greatly appreciate the financial support for much of this research which was provided by an International Doctoral Research Fellowship from the Social Science Research Council, by a grant from the Wenner-Gren Foundation for Anthropological Research, and by a Postdoctoral Research Training Fellowship from the Social Science Research Council.

This study would not have been possible without the cooperation of a great many people in Wales, and I gratefully acknowledge their contributions. Many individuals went well beyond the requirements of a formal interview to offer encouragement, help, and advice, and I thank them for their interest in this research.

Acknowledgment is due to Richard G. Fox, who guided my research in its early stages. I would also like to express my appreciation for the facilities and expertise provided by Gwynedd Information Technology Centre, Caernarfon, during the preparation of the index and to the staff of the National Library of Wales for their assistance with bibliographic details.

Finally, I would like to thank my husband, Hywel Davies, for his personal encouragement and professional assistance throughout the years of my involvement in this research. Without his help, this study would never have been completed.

Any errors or omissions that remain are entirely my own responsibility.

Charlotte Aull Davies
January 1989

Welsh Nationalism
in the Twentieth Century

1

Theoretical and Historical Background

Separatist political movements that challenge the territorial integrity of the presumed well-integrated states of the First World have been a major, if unanticipated, political force in the second half of the twentieth century. These movements, which are defined by ethnic differences and draw upon nationalist ideology, may be found in virtually every state in Western Europe and North America,[1] from the Breton and Corsican movements in a highly centralized France to the movement for provincial status in the Jura in decentralized Switzerland. A few have achieved notable success, for example, the Basques in northern Spain who have had their own parliament, with considerable autonomy, since 1980. Most have been less successful in forcing fundamental reorganization of the existing state; the Parti Quebecois, for example, has seen its ultimate goal of separation from the Canadian state rejected in a popular referendum. [See C. R. Foster (1980), Rokkan and Urwin (1982), and Tiryakian and Rogowski (1985) for studies of a range of such movements.] The majority of such movements, nevertheless, have gained some concessions or achieved administrative reforms beneficial to the ethnic region. Such gains have seldom been insignificant; on the contrary, they have commonly been relatively costly for the central state (Rudolph & Thompson, 1985).

The Scottish and Welsh nationalist movements in Great Britain, while differing from one another in many respects, have followed roughly similar paths: a flurry of internal activity with some limited electoral success in the immediate post–World War II years; two decades of quiescence; some significant electoral advances in the late 1960s and early 1970s; a steep decline following the Referenda on Assemblies for Scotland and Wales in 1979; and some limited indications of a revival in the late 1980s. Yet despite the fluctuations in the appeal of separatist politics, the basis for such appeals remained relatively constant. In the general election of 1987, Scottish and Welsh voters made clearly separate, if not explicitly separatist, political choices when compared to voters in England; in the three general elections from 1979 to 1987, in which nearly 50 percent of the voters of southern England and the English midlands supported the Conservative Party to give it very large parliamentary majorities, over 40 percent of the voters in Scotland and Wales supported the Labour Party and the 1987 Tory vote was below 30 percent (see *The Times*, 13 June 1987). Furthermore, such political behavior represented a long-established pattern in which significant differences in electoral decisions between the Celtic areas and the core area of Britain have been shown to persist even after the effects of socioeconomic differences between the core and periphery have been removed (Hechter, 1975). Analysis of these ethnically based separatist movements suggests that their political viability has not disappeared. They will reemerge periodically until minority nationalisms achieve a more satisfactory accommodation in the international order (cf. Nagel, 1984; Richmond, 1984).

ETHNIC NATIONALISM: THEORETICAL PERSPECTIVE

Ethnic nationalist movements are found in areas that are peripheral to the main seat of government and of administration of the central state. Their leaders can point to a period, mostly in the distant past, though occasionally relatively recently, when these regions were recognizably separate entities with cultural and social, although not always political, unity. They were acquired, whether by conquest, dictat, or mutual agreement, by an expanding neighbor in process of becoming the core region of a nascent state. While politically a part of these newly evolving states, the peripheral regions remained culturally distinct from the core, except for their upwardly (and often outwardly) mobile elites. Nor was there any pressure on them to do otherwise. Early state formations resembled ancient empires in what they expected from their acquired territories, namely, revenue, manpower for their armies, and, sometimes, buffer lands at their frontiers to dispense to various categories of followers. But such states had neither interest in nor means of influencing social and cultural mores among the majority of inhabitants; thus, language, family arrangements, agricultural patterns, and social institutions of all kinds were virtually unaffected by the state. Although the degree of interference by the central state gradually increased as monarchs tried to improve efficiency of administration to increase revenues, a major change in the position of peripheral cultures occurred during the eighteenth century with the coincidence of two interrelated phenomena, the Industrial Revolution and the rise of the new and powerful ideology of nationalism.

The Industrial Revolution fundamentally altered the economic relationship of a peripheral area with the core, particularly if that region contained raw materials needed to fuel the new industries. The degree to which wealth was siphoned from the region and accumulated in the core and the manner in which the entire regional substructure, both material and social, was transformed to facilitate this transfer of wealth represented a qualitative change in the relationship between core and periphery. At the same time, the cultural differences between core and periphery were reinforced in the economic organization; indeed the cultural differences were commonly taken as an explanation for the economic disadvantage of the ethnic region.

In this same period, and linked to the growth of industrial capitalism, a new ideology was propounded which gave a previously unheard of political significance to cultural differences. Nationalism adopted the concept of rightful sovereignty from the doctrine of enlightened monarchy, but contended that such sovereignty, rather than being invested in the monarch, was inherent in the collectivity of individuals composing the nation. The state was the political representation of the nation, sovereign over its territory by consent of the governed. Given this basis for political organization, the unity of the state was no longer a matter of loyalty to a monarch, its personification, but was based on the unity of a collection of individuals making up the nation. The rationalization for such unity was sought in common culture, most often defined by common history or language (A. D. Smith, 1971, 1981). Thus, for the first time, the legitimacy of the state ultimately rested, in theory at least, on individual assumptions about cultural identity and on individual priorities as to which of alternative cultural identities to emphasize in determining political loyalties. The existence of a 'nation-state' was problematic, based on whether or not a given collectivity considered themselves to constitute a nation and hence accepted the legitimacy of the state's authority.

Recognition of this major shift in the ideological basis for the legitimacy of the state should not obscure the real locus of economic and political power in the states that developed under nationalist ideology. These emerging 'nation-states' were clearly controlled by the industrial and commercial middle classes which arose throughout Western Europe with the development of industrial capitalism. Nevertheless, basing the authority of the state, even in part, on such an ideology had far-reaching consequences. The concept that the state's right to govern derives ultimately from the consent of the people has been the basis of campaigns for increased political justice and social equality in the liberal democracies of the West since the late eighteenth century. While nationalist ideology cannot be credited as the principal force behind the advances made in these areas, it has proven a powerful ideological ally.[2] Nationalism also provided the theoretical basis of struggles for independence in the former colonial areas of the Third World. This same ideology, that state authority properly rests on national representation, has been and will continue to be applied to ethnic regions in long-established states, where political separatist movements claim nationhood status by virtue of historical association, cultural unity, and ultimately self-definition.

Because the legitimating ideology of 'nation-states' relied so heavily on historical continuity of identity and possession of a common culture, the activities of the state were often directed toward discounting historical divisions and cultural differences within its own borders. As transportation and communication networks improved, the potential for increased supervision meant also a potential for increased control over areas of life that had been outside the purview of the state. In particular, states became concerned to ensure cultural homogeneity of the populations under their sway, both as a source of legitimation of rule and as a means of making supervision still easier. Measures promoting uniformity in language, law, administrative arrangements, and a host of social customs and cultural markers were gradually introduced.

Given the general effectiveness of these overt measures as well as of the more diffuse forces of modernization, theoreticians came to expect that the populations of the 'nation-states' of Western Europe were becoming genuinely homogenized. Thus modernization theory predicted the gradual disappearance of status groups within state boundaries, and of the political separatist sympathies which drew on them, and their replacement by functional identities of occupation and class (Gordon, 1975; Tiryakian, 1980). Other similar diffusionist theories, with a different disciplinary orientation, tried to measure the degree to which cultural homogeneity had been achieved by looking at inventories of culture traits, although such acculturation studies tended to concentrate on immigrant ethnic groups rather than ethnic populations in a region which they had historically occupied (e.g., Gans, 1962; Whyte, 1955). However, the political events of the late 1960s and early 1970s made it clear that a narrowing of the differences in terms of culture traits between ethnic and majority populations did not imply a loss of ethnic identity nor a loss of the basis for separatist political movements (Glazer & Moynihan, 1975).

The first major alternative theoretical treatment of ethnic groups in modern states contended that regional ethnic differences were due to the mode of economic integration of the region into the state (Hechter, 1975). Ethnic nationalist movements were said to be a reaction to the exploitation of the ethnic region as a result of its being essentially an internal colony of

Theoretical and Historical Background

the state. The economic organization of these internal colonies was a cultural division of labor, whereby an ethnic working class, which was usually concentrated in one or two extractive industries, contributed disproportionately to the wealth of the central state and its capitalist class. Ethnic regions which experienced this form of economic integration into the state also tended toward distinctive political behavior with occasional bursts of explicitly separatist demands.

While the concept of a cultural division of labor was clearly valid for many ethnic regions, others, also with quite strong ethnic nationalist movements, could not be accurately described as internal colonies. Many of these had begun to establish a native industrial capitalist base prior to their integration into the larger state system, and some were actually relatively advantaged with respect to the core area. The economic organization in these regions, a modification of the theory contended, was a vertical segmentation in which members of the ethnic group monopolized particular occupational niches, rather than a horizontal cultural division of labor (Hechter & Levi, 1979). A political separatist response occurred with the intrusion of nonethnics into these ethnically controlled economic segments. Clearly such a theory resembled earlier diffusion theories and has indeed been called a diffusion competition model.

It might be expected that ethnic regions characterized by the diffusion competition model would still be likely to succumb eventually to forces of modernization, once the areas of ethnic control were finally penetrated. Certainly the removal of such ethnic hegemony would seem more likely in these regions than in those fitting the internal colonial, or reactive ethnicity, model: in the former regions, the areas of ethnic control are presumably desirable economic niches, offering prospects for vertical advancement within that segment; in those regions with a cultural division of labor, the strata reserved for ethnics is a horizontal layer at the bottom of the economic structure, one that nonethnics are less likely to covet. However, another factor gives the ethnic regions in the diffusion competition model considerable endurance and ability to withstand dilution. Such regions are usually in possession of a relatively extensive organizational framework. When, as in Scotland, law, education, even banking, have organizations based on the ethnic region, then these areas of hegemony are quite difficult for outsiders to penetrate, due in large measure to their lack of expertise in fields where insider knowledge and even access to training is controlled by ethnics. Usually, such regions were incorporated relatively recently into the state on somewhat more equal terms than those that were acquired, often by conquest, at an earlier date and that became internal colonies. The ethnic organizational framework of regions with a cultural division of labor, by comparison, is usually very meagre; Welsh organizations do not encompass vital social and economic institutions, such as law and banking, and they are virtually all quite recent, dating from the 1960s and 1970s, the period of nationalist resurgence and electoral successes. Thus the differences in the two models that describe ethnic regions also imply quite fundamental differences in the bases of the sense of ethnic regional separateness associated with each; these differences are reflected in ideological emphasis, methods, strengths, and weaknesses of their political nationalist movements.

These two models account quite adequately for the maintenance of ethnic identity and sentiment in peripheral regions of 'nation-states' and for the consistent differences in political expression between such peripheral areas and the core areas of the state. However, their highly structural level of analysis limits their explanatory ability with respect to the variations in separatist movements within these ethnic regions (Hechter, 1985). While the level of ethnic sentiment or identity remained relatively constant, the strength and appeal of ethnic nationalist political parties fluctuated quite radically in the twentieth century. Thus, explanations of the timing, intensity, and character of such movements are to be found at a different level of analysis from that of these purely structural theories.

Theories of group solidarity and collective action have been suggested as a viable basis for analyzing the sporadic appearances and varying strength of political separatist movements (Hechter, Friedman, & Appelbaum, 1982). Such theories direct attention to individual calculations to evaluate likely gains and losses from pursuing a particular course of action. Individuals are presumed to be rational actors who do not take action unless they perceive a personal advantage can thereby be secured. Thus attention is directed to decision-making processes whereby a disorganized collection of individuals is persuaded to act in concert to further collective ends. A major concern of this theoretical orientation then becomes explaining how a group overcomes the so-called free-rider dilemma. The free-rider dilemma refers to the argument that most group action, and certainly political movements, are engaged primarily in reaching goals that will produce 'public goods,' that is, goods which, once achieved, are available to all whether or not they participated in the movement that produced them. Thus the rational actor will not undertake collective action, at an individual cost, when the only benefits accruing from such action will be available equally to all members of the society whether or not they participated in the collective action. Barring idiosyncratic responses, the majority of individuals will participate in collective action only if they can thereby also obtain private benefits, whether material or nonmaterial, not available to nonparticipants. The free-rider dilemma helps explain the relative rarity of collective action, given that effective action depends on a group being able to offer immediate and relatively certain rewards to participants beyond participation in the pursuit of a worthy goal, whose realization in any case may be evaluated by participants as highly improbable. A group's success at collective action is further dependent on its ability to sanction behavior by its members which does not further its goals or which deviates from its expectations. Thus individual calculations of whether or not to participate in collective action may be said to be based on these factors: the private rewards accruing to the individual if the group is successful; the private rewards to be gained by the individual regardless of group success; the losses likely to be incurred from participation in the group action; and the sanctions likely to be imposed by the group if the individual does not act as expected. In addition, all of these factors are weighted by the estimated probability of their occurrence (Hardin, 1982; Hechter, 1983; Olson, 1971).

While such an explanation appears to move the analysis to the opposite extreme from the structural explanations that have dominated the analyses of ethnic nationalist political movements, two considerations make the divide much less than it initially appears. First, while the analysis is concerned with individual decision making, such decision-making processes as are of interest are those that are representative of categories of individuals. While the theory does not discount the possibility of some individuals making decisions on bases not amenable to analysis by a rational calculus, these are outside the province of the explanation. The theory argues that most individuals most of the time make such rational calculations, working within the framework of the information available to them, as a basis for their decisions and that individuals in similar structural positions arrive at similar decisions. Thus while the theory does not attempt to explain the actions of the occasional martyr or charismatic leader, it can help account for the actions of the groups that coalesce around them. [See Adam (1984), Dickie-Clark (1984), and Hechter and Friedman (1984a, 1984b) for debate on the application of rational-choice theory.]

Any analysis of collective action must recognize that individuals contemplating involvement in such action can select from a spectrum of choices representing various degrees of commitment. In a political separatist movement these choices range from a high level of activism involving considerable individual cost and high visibility, to the virtually invisible and low-cost act of voting for a separatist political party. It is assumed that the decision-making processes of individuals in similar structural positions at each of these various levels can be analyzed as a category in order to understand the success or otherwise of collective action in its various aspects, from recruiting leaders to winning votes in elections (cf. Levi & Hechter, 1985).

A second link between analyses based on the theory of collective action and structural levels of explanation is to be found in those factors that influence individual decision making (cf. Nielsen, 1985, for one application of this approach). Structural theories have called attention to the socioeconomic conditions that support distinct ethnic identities in peripheral regions. These conditions maintain the potential for separatist political movements based on ethnic distinctiveness to develop. However, such generalized conditions cannot directly enter into an individual's decision-making equation; instead individuals respond to specific factors deriving from these conditions which may persuade them to commit themselves to group action. For example, changes in the state, in particular the growth of the welfare state, certainly seem to be associated with the politicization of ethnic identities (Aull, 1979; Enloe, 1981; Fox, Aull, & Cimino, 1980; van Amersfoort & van der Wusten, 1981). However, the fluctuations in ethnic nationalist movements occur as individuals respond to specific aspects of state activity and determine to support, as activists or voters, an ethnic political organization. By differentiating general structural causes and relating specific factors to individual choices an analysis of the pattern of successes and failures of ethnic nationalist movements becomes possible.

ETHNIC NATIONALISM IN BRITAIN

In Great Britain four major regions can lay claim to a separate cultural identity from the dominant culture centered in the southeast of England: Scotland, the north of England, Wales, and Cornwall (cf. Urwin, 1982). Of these, Scotland stands apart in the manner and timing of its absorption by the British state. It was integrated by treaty at a relatively late date, 1707, by which time it already had a native capitalist class, as well as a number of Scottish organizations and institutions in areas of considerable significance. Scottish law required the maintenance of a separate Scottish legal system; the Scottish educational system through the university level remained separate from that of England; the Bank of Scotland issued its own currency; and Scottish Presbyterianism, which developed independently of Protestantism in England, retained its separate organization. These organizational reinforcements of Scottish identity meant that Scottish culture did not carry the primary burden of maintaining a separate Scottish identity. Furthermore, the fact that Scotland was not incorporated as an internal colony meant that Scottish cultural identity never suffered the denigration or the association with economic failure that is an inherent part of an economic organization based on a cultural division of labor.

Wales, the north of England, and Cornwall were all incorporated by an expanding English state in an earlier epoch. The subjugation of these regions extended over several centuries but was substantially completed by the sixteenth century (cf. Bulpitt, 1983). Wales, the most difficult to subdue, was officially absorbed by the Act of Union of 1536. All three of these regions contained raw materials vital to the new industries that developed in the eighteenth and nineteenth centuries and all became economic internal colonies in Britain. The type and degree of economic exploitation in the three regions were very similar, yet Wales was the only one of the three to develop a political separatist movement that can be compared in strength and effectiveness to that in Scotland. An ethnic nationalist party did appear in Cornwall, and there was some poorly developed separatist sentiment in the north of England. However, neither region had a separatist movement with any real electoral strength or significant organization. Wales, in contrast, had a nationalist party from 1925 onwards; Plaid Cymru (the name used by the Welsh Nationalist Party from 1945) elected its first Member of Parliament in a by-election in 1966, and in 1987 had three MPs, out of a Welsh total of 38. In local government, in 1987, the Blaid[3] was either the strongest party (with independents in control) or the main opposition party on two county councils and five district councils. The party attracted nearly 12 percent of the total vote in the general election of 1970; this high value had fallen to 7 percent by 1987 (see Figure 1.1). In comparison to the Scottish Nationalist Party, Plaid Cymru was generally weaker, yet the two parties represented a significant force in British political life. They, and the nationalist movements of which

Figure 1.1
Plaid Cymru Electoral History, General Elections 1945–1987

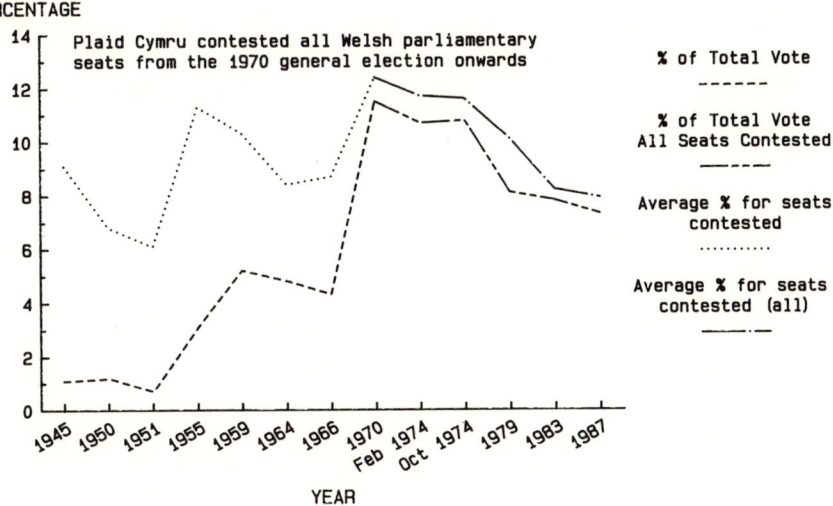

Sources: Craig (1969, 1976);
Dods Parliamentary Companion (1950–1987)

they were a part, retained, in the late twentieth century, the potential to alter fundamentally the structure of the British state.

Given the strong organizational basis of a separate Scottish identity, the successes of the Scottish Nationalist Party are easier to understand. In Wales from the time of the Act of Union in 1536, the British state had a deliberate policy of eradicating all cultural and organizational bases of Welsh identity. The Welsh language was banned from all official use and, with the coming of universal education, attacked in the schools. All separate Welsh organizations had been successfully eliminated by the end of the eighteenth century; and the structure of at least one institution imposed after union, that of the circuit courts, was divisive in that it attached Monmouthshire in the southeast corner of Wales to an English circuit. The only structural reinforcement for Welsh identity was that inherent in a cultural division of labor. While a powerful enforcer of ethnic identity from outside, this economic structure was not an inducement for nationalist action. On the contrary, it presented a strong incentive for an identity switch, from the denigrated ethnic identity so closely associated with economic and social failure to that of the majority culture. Thus the case of Welsh nationalism is particularly challenging and potentially informative in that understanding its progression in the twentieth century involves analyzing the combination of particular structural forces, internal ethnic resources, and group rewards and sanctions that produced a viable movement for national political independence. These factors combined to produce nationalist leaders and activists as well as a favorable electoral response from a significant, though always far from a majority, segment of the population.

WELSH NATIONALISM: NINETEENTH-CENTURY ROOTS

The nationalist movement of the twentieth century was not the first political movement in Wales to be based on cultural distinctiveness and to appeal to nationalist ideology. Beginning about 1850 and extending through the second half of the nineteenth century, major changes in Welsh society and politics occurred which cumulatively constituted a nationalist movement, broadly interpreted. This movement expressed itself politically through the British Liberal Party, with only a very brief and quickly aborted attempt to form a separate political party with explicitly nationalist goals. In many respects, nineteenth-century Welsh nationalism was a blind alley rather than a genuine predecessor to the twentieth-century movement. Its legacy, in terms of image and issues, proved more hindrance than help by the mid-twentieth century; and it left no political organization on which a new nationalist movement could be based. However, the movement succeeded in establishing a few important national institutions, including a national university, and it gained a modicum of official recognition for Welsh unity by obtaining some legislation applicable only to Wales. Changes in the British state provided the major structural stimulant both for nineteenth-century Welsh nationalism and for the twentieth-century movement, but the nature of these changes and the nationalist responses to them were very different in the two periods.

By the mid-nineteenth century, one of the major cultural markers and the only organizational basis of Welsh identity was provided by the nonconformist churches, that is, the protestant denominations that had broken away from or formed outside of the established Anglican Church. While the nonconformist denominations enjoyed notable success among the industrial working classes throughout Britain, they were particularly successful in Wales, being adopted both by rural and by urban working classes. Since most anglicized landowners retained their Anglican Church affiliation and since the nonconformist chapels were further differentiated from Anglicanism by their use of the Welsh language, nonconformity became closely associated with Welshness. And the democratically organized chapels began to produce a new, community-based elite and a Welsh middle class (cf. Verdery, 1976).

Historically, the developing states of Western Europe had seen a major challenge to their authority coming from the Church of Rome; in some instances, monarchs responded to this external threat by usurping the authority and wealth of the Church within their own boundaries. In Britain, a state church, with the monarch as head, was established in the sixteenth century. By the nineteenth century, the state church received compulsory tithes, registered births, deaths, and marriages, determined place of burial, and was a major provider of education and social welfare. While these powers were not wielded directly by the central state, the full authority of the state stood behind their possession by the Anglican Church. Such involvement by the state in everyday life was extraordinary for a period when there was no central state income tax nor provision for education or health.

The nonconformist denominations did not pose a threat to the authority of the state, but the control wielded by the state church over many social institutions was a source of frustration for their members. Given the highly sectarian character of nonconformity, cooperation among the various denominations was difficult to attain. However, aided by the Liberation Society, a British organization opposed to state religion, they eventually coalesced around the issue of disestablishment of the Anglican Church, with other religious issues (Sunday closing of pubs, church-controlled education) also playing a part. Thus the central issue for Welsh nationalism in the nineteenth century was the encroachment of the state, in the form of the state church, into everyday individual concerns. The proposed solution was the dispossession of the Anglican Church of such powers over Welsh society and their elimination or transfer to secular authorities.

Both the central issue and the means for addressing it sprang from state structure. As polity modernization, in the form of a gradual extension of the franchise, was forced upon the state elite during the course of the century, the new Welsh nonconformist elite replaced conservative Anglican representatives in parliament and in local government. Working within the British Liberal Party, they sought solutions for nonconformist concerns in the form of new legislation. They succeeded in obtaining special legislation for Wales, in particular the Welsh Sunday Closing Act and the Welsh Intermediate Education Act. But they did not achieve their main goal, disestablishment, until 1919, by which time Liberal nonconformist Welsh nationalism was being seriously challenged by the labor movement.

The structural positions of the Welsh nonconformist elite explain both the goals they pursued and the eventual demise of the nationalist movement they created. Two distinct Welsh elites can be identified in this period. The first group constituted a community elite, principally the ministers and deacons of nonconformist chapels. The highly localized nature of Welsh culture, reflected and bolstered by the organization of Welsh nonconformity into individual chapels each with great autonomy, discouraged the development of a national Welsh identity. Furthermore, the communication and transportation infrastructure was insufficient to support the sort of national network required for the sustenance of such a Welsh identity. However, one group, consisting mainly of Members of Parliament and other prominent Welshmen living in London, was in a position to develop such an identity, and these individuals came to constitute a national elite. These individuals had occasion to travel about the country, to develop contacts with one another and hence to participate in a national social network. [See Jenkins and Ramage (1951) for a history of one of their most influential organizations.] Another factor contributing to the development of a national Welsh identity among this group was their daily association with English society where their Welsh identity was highly salient but any finer distinctions as to local origins within Wales were irrelevant.

In the final decade of the nineteenth century, a few among the national Welsh elite attempted to move away from the British Liberal Party and establish a genuine nationalist movement demanding separate political institutions for Wales. Led by David Lloyd George, this group intended to make Cymru Fydd (Wales to Be) an umbrella organization for the movement which would absorb both the North and South Wales Liberal Federations. Cymru Fydd had been established in London and Liverpool primarily as a cultural and literary organization, and although it had many branches in Wales, its membership was far from unanimous in support of nationalist political goals. A major reason for the lack of substantial grassroots support for this movement was the greater importance of local identities over Welsh identity and the low salience of Welsh political goals for the community elite whose support made possible other Liberal nonconformist political achievements (cf. R.T. Jenkins, 1935). The demise of Cymru Fydd, even as a national elite coalition, occurred in a dispute between Lloyd George, whose power base was in north Wales, and leaders of the South Wales Liberals, who maintained that the industrial counties of south Wales would be unfairly dominated by rural north and mid-Wales in any such all-Wales organization (Grigg, 1973; K. O. Morgan, 1963). The defeat of this attempt at nationalist organization was due both to the group's inability to sanction members' behavior and the paucity of private rewards it could make available. A large segment of the national Welsh elite, including D. A. Thomas, Lloyd George's principal opponent in south Wales, had supported nationalist goals at some time in their careers. While many of them could visualize leadership positions for themselves once separate Welsh institutions were set up, the rewards on the path to separatism were scarce and collective action toward such an end involved risking already established positions in the British Liberal Party. Most, including Lloyd George after 1896, determined that it was more rational to pursue careers within the Liberal Party with its rewards for faithful service and sanctions against those who broke party ranks.

Thus the legacy of nineteenth-century Welsh nationalism for the twentieth-century movement was mixed, essential to its development in some respects, harmful to its prospects of ever becoming a mass movement in others. The most important achievement of Liberal Welsh nationalism was its establishment of some national institutions. The University of Wales, a national library, and a national museum were all products of the late nineteenth century. An additional achievement was the creation, in 1906, of a Welsh Department of the Board of Education. However, in its basic political and social organization Wales remained undifferentiated from England. Nor was any political organization established that could provide a platform from which to launch a future nationalist campaign. Furthermore, the nonconformist issues that so dominated Liberal Welsh nationalism became increasingly irrelevant in political life as the labor movement began to assume more importance. Yet the image of Welsh nationalists as middle-class, chapel-going teetotallers would survive and prove difficult to dislodge from a later nationalist movement whose character would be quite different.

Another important contribution of the nineteenth century to twentieth-century Welsh nationalism was the primacy that the national elite gave to their Welsh identity, over that based on their communities of origin, and their contention that the existence of this distinct Welsh identity created separate Welsh issues in many British political debates. The increased political salience of Welsh identity, which they managed to achieve, was manifest in its use by the labor movement in Wales as it struggled to wrest political power from the Liberals in the early decades of the twentieth century. Whereas nonconformity did not play a significant role in the political rhetoric of labor candidates, Welsh nationality certainly did. Keir Hardie, the first labor MP from Wales, was a supporter of Welsh national identity and argued that it could contribute to the socialist cause (K. O. Morgan, 1966). In the years just prior to World War I, several prominent members of the Independent Labour Party tried to obtain official recognition for Wales within their party and wrote of the union of nationalism and socialism in Welsh politics (D. H. Davies, 1983, pp. 10–12). However, as the political dominance of the British Labour Party over Wales was strengthened in the 1920s and 1930s, the importance of Welsh nationality in political rhetoric declined. The Labour Party looked to centralization on British lines to alleviate the extreme economic hardship of the depression, and many in the Labour Party, of whom Aneurin Bevan was the most notable example, were very hostile to any suggestion that there were particular Welsh interests divorced from Britain as a whole. Nevertheless, even in this period of centralist emphasis, a few Welsh Labour MPs retained their interest in Welsh national identity as a political factor, and some of these came into prominence in the 1940s and 1950s favoring formal bureaucratic recognition for Wales (K. O. Morgan, 1982, pp. 297–299).

However, by that time, a rival as defender of Welsh national interests had entered political life. The Welsh Nationalist Party had been struggling, since its foundation in 1925, to create an identity distinct from nineteenth-century liberalism and to build a viable political nationalist movement. By the mid-1940s the party, still very weak in electoral terms, was showing some signs of political vitality. The existence and subsequent successes of Plaid Cymru (the Party of Wales), as it had begun to call itself, would fundamentally alter political debate for all parties in Wales.

WELSH NATIONALISM: THE TWENTIETH CENTURY

Welsh nationalism in the twentieth century drew upon the heightened consciousness of Welsh nationality that was a product of the nationalist movement of the previous century. And like its predecessor, the new nationalism responded to major changes in the British state: the nationalist movement of the nineteenth century was facilitated by polity modernization and that of the twentieth century by certain aspects of state modernization. However, they differed fundamentally in the ethnic resources on which they primarily drew and in the manner in which they employed such resources. The bases on which a viable modern nationalist movement were reconstructed were history, language, economic organization, and bureaucracy, each of which provided a major focus of nationalist activity. Structural factors determined which of these foci were preeminent in different periods, while group dynamics further affected its character and degree of success.

Nothing so distinguishes the two nationalist movements in Wales as their respective manner of utilizing the basic national resources of history and language. While the nineteenth-century nationalist movement had drawn primarily on nonconformity for its issues, image, and personnel, the national (London-based) Welsh elite had also concerned themselves with these other areas of Welsh culture. Since English society, rather than a Welsh constituency, provided the primary audience for a large segment of this elite, one of their major concerns was to demonstrate that Wales had contributed to England's cultural eminence and imperial greatness. To this end they nourished a highly romanticized view of Welsh history whose culmination was the assumption of the English crown by the Welshman Henry Tudor (Henry VII) in 1485. The first indication of an altered nationalist movement developing in Wales was the redefinition and rewriting of Welsh history begun in the early decades of the twentieth century. Welsh national historians eschewed looking at Wales primarily in terms of its relationship to England and, by recovering and reinterpreting events that had been ignored or given very different treatment by English-oriented historians, created a history of and for the Welsh nation. This fundamental shift in the treatment of the history of Wales altered the ideological basis of Welsh nationalism; it played a central role in the early stages of nationalist elite recruitment but had only a minor part in the development of a mass movement. Welsh historians continued to reflect, and support, shifts in emphasis within the nationalist movement in the 1970s and 1980s with their growing interest in social history and the Welsh working class.

Similarly, nationalists in the twentieth century fundamentally altered the significance and role of the Welsh language in the nationalist movement. In the nineteenth century, the Welsh national elite had made limited use of the language to gain legislation particularly for Wales in the area of education, but they had done so by treating it as a handicap to be overcome. A completely different perspective on the significance of the Welsh language produced, in the twentieth century, successful campaigns for official recognition of its status and for the provision of schools which used it as their primary medium of instruction. The interaction of structural factors and group dynamics in the language movement made it, in one period, the leading edge of the nationalist movement. Furthermore, it continued to be a very important resource for the political nationalist movement as a whole, a central role which was maintained in spite of the divisive forces inherent in the mixed linguistic situation extant in Wales by the mid-twentieth century.

The two nationalist movements also differed fundamentally in their relationship with the economic and bureaucratic structures of the state. Both nineteenth- and twentieth-century Welsh elites struggled with the negative stereotype of Welshness generated by the relationships inherent under a cultural division of labor. The solution of the London Welsh in the nineteenth century was to ignore industrial Wales and encourage depictions of the Welsh as a pastoral people occupying a semimagical land of Celtic romance. Nationalists in the twentieth century, aspiring to create a mass movement, had to face the consequences for Welsh identity of this form of economic exploitation. However, they too found a realistic response elusive, especially in the early decades of the nationalist party. Party founders and members in the 1920s and 1930s had their own reasons for revaluing Welsh culture, and their energies were concentrated in this area with little being done to address the economic powerlessness that lay at the roots of impoverishment and cultural denigration. Even their criticisms of the British state were motivated primarily by cultural rather than economic causes (D. H. Davies, 1983). Changes in the state in the post–World War II years eventually provided the structural stimulus for a major change in the character of the nationalist movement, increasing both the importance of economics in nationalist politics and the prospects for the party to attract a mass following.

Although both the nineteenth- and twentieth-century nationalist movements were stimulated by changes in the British state, the general nature of the changes in the two periods was quite different. In the nineteenth century, the nationalist movement was facilitated by electoral reform, and nationalists pursued their nonconformist-dominated goals almost exclusively through the legislative system. Twentieth-century nationalists, lacking in significant influence over the legislative process, found other opportunities in the bureaucratic expansion that accompanied the growth of the welfare state in the post–World War II era. The growth of the welfare bureaucracy was of general benefit to the broader nationalist movement because of the opportunity it provided for the creation of Welsh organizations, giving Wales a degree of the official institutional reinforcement of Welsh identity long enjoyed by Scotland. The recognition of Welsh identity in bureaucratic organization was not a foregone conclusion. Basing their arguments primarily on Welsh culture in the first instance and later on administrative precedent, nationalists were successful in winning such recognition over a period of two decades, culminating in 1964 with the creation of the Welsh Office as a separate department of the central government. Once begun, such an infrastructure had considerable vitality of its own, stimulating the development of other Welsh organizations within the bureaucracy as well as in nongovernmental realms having extensive dealings with the state, such as trade unions.

While Welsh organization in virtually any sphere added to the institutional reinforcement of Welsh identity, not all areas were of equal significance for political nationalist organization or for nationalist electoral support. A critical factor in the relationship between political nationalism and the growth of the welfare state was the greatly expanded role of the state in economic planning. An increase in state activity in this area created the potential that Wales might be constituted an economic unit for planning purposes. Just such a possibility arose in the 1940s when the government began to introduce economic measures to avoid a repeat of the drastic deflation that had followed World War I. However, nationalists were unable to secure any significant economic organization for Wales at that time; what occurred was a flurry of demands for Welsh economic structures followed by the strengthening of the British-based economic system both in nationalized industries and the trade unions. The possibility of creating Welsh economic structures appeared again in the late 1960s, when regional planning on a broad geographic scale was introduced to redress regional economic imbalances. By this time, the complex of Welsh organizations that had been created with the Welsh Office at the core was sufficiently influential within the state bureaucracy to ensure that this new era of economic planning would treat Wales as a unit. The Welsh Office was given responsibility for economic planning for Wales and a Welsh Development Agency was set up in 1976. Furthermore, the encouragement of a Welsh economic structure from within the bureaucracy soon stimulated the restructuring along Welsh lines of the major organization representing business interests and, more significantly, of the trade union movement: both a Welsh branch of the Confederation of British Industry and a Trades Union Council for Wales were established in the 1970s.

The political nationalist movement showed its greatest vitality in the late 1940s and again in the late 1960s, with much more sustained growth occurring in the latter period. And the changes within Plaid Cymru were linked to the developments in the bureaucracy favoring Welsh economic unity. In both periods the Blaid attracted activists whose political outlook diverged from that of the existing party leadership, particularly in their greater interest in economic issues. And these new activists were able to alter electoral tactics and affect policy development. Particularly in the latter period, nationalist political development was fundamentally redirected, leading eventually to the flowering of a strong socialist position within the nationalist party. In electoral terms, there was only a slight indication of increased popular appeal for the party in the earlier period of the 1940s. However, the late 1960s and 1970s produced important nationalist successes at the polls; nor were these gains entirely lost as the Blaid's fortunes began to decline from about 1978 onwards.

While many aspects of state modernization were positive resources for the nationalist movement, some had a negative impact. One such was the increasing importance of the mass media in political campaigns. Television, in particular, tended to reflect statewide issues at the expense of regional concerns and concentrated interest on the leaders of the major British parties rather than on local candidates. Political rallies and meetings and political literature had much less impact by the 1980s than in the 1940s: they affected only those voters with a relatively active interest in politics; most ignored them in favor of television news presentations where minority party access was normally limited. Under such conditions a minority party, particularly one whose constituency was restricted to a specific geographic region, had great difficulty ensuring that its message was heard at all.

Popular referenda also proved an effective weapon against separatist movements in several instances, notably in Scotland and Wales in 1979 and in Quebec in 1980. The Labour government's proposal for an elected assembly for Wales, to which Plaid Cymru became heavily committed, was defeated in a referendum, and this setback precipitated a period of demoralization and disorganization in Welsh political nationalism. Although the broader nationalist movement found other avenues of expression, nationalist electoral effectiveness was seriously damaged, and Plaid Cymru had not recovered its former political vitality by the mid-1980s. Even in Scotland, where the devolution proposal was passed but not by the majority required for implementation, the nationalist movement was seriously damaged; in fact, nationalists in Scotland suffered proportionately much heavier losses than in Wales in the general election that followed the referendum. The 1979 referenda and subsequent general election clearly marked the end of the nationalist resurgence that had begun in Wales and Scotland in the mid-1960s. The negative impact of the referenda upon these nationalist movements derived from structural changes underway when they were introduced, primarily the pulling back from the commitment to the welfare state as it had developed since World War II. Decisions made by Plaid Cymru specifically relating to the Assembly campaign as well as the conflicting responses of several groups within the Labour Party also influenced the outcome.

SUMMARY

The course of the nationalist movement in Wales has been determined by the interaction of structural forces emanating primarily from changes in the British state, with the microsociological processes of individual decision making. Various categories of individuals responded to specific structural changes by becoming involved in nationalist activity at some level, as political activist, as cultural nationalist, or as a voter. Their own structural positions and their interactions both with nationalist groups and other social groupings determined the form and extent of their involvement.

There have been four major focal areas for nationalist involvement in this century, namely, national history, the Welsh language, the economy, and the British bureaucracy. The first focus, which began to differentiate twentieth-century nationalism from that of the Liberal nonconformist nationalism of the preceding century, was that of creating a national history for Wales. This was mainly an elitist activity and was facilitated by very different structural factors from those of the second major nationalist focus, namely, the much more broadly based, but still relatively apolitical, Welsh language movement. The expansion of the state bureaucracy into areas affecting economic life was closely associated with improvements in the electoral performance of Plaid Cymru as well as with changes in the character of party membership and consequent internal policy developments. However, the effectiveness of the political nationalist focus on the Welsh economy was dependent upon the processes of administrative devolution that established Wales as a unit within the British bureaucracy. Furthermore, the degree of bureaucratic recognition for Wales was critical for other focal areas of nationalist activity as well.

In the chapters that follow, the development of each of these nationalist foci is analyzed as the outcome of individual decision-making processes informed and influenced by a combination of structural forces and group dynamics. The explanations thus developed represent an intermediate level of generalization in social theory. Although such a theory cannot be transferred in its entirety to nationalist movements in other locations, it contains clusters of explanatory factors that are applicable to other movements, and such application provides a further test of its validity. The concluding chapter explores some of these areas of application to other nationalist movements.

NOTES

1. While ethnically based political movements in the United States, in particular the Black civil rights movement, may be regarded as a form of ethnic nationalism,

they lack an explicit separatist component in that they, unlike the historic nationalities of Western Europe, have no clear territorial base. The campaigns of some Native American groups to regain tribal lands or to increase their autonomy on such lands provide a closer parallel to the territorially based movements discussed herein. It is worthy of note that the Soviet Union, with its incorporated nationalities and its large and intrusive bureaucracy, also appears to provide scope for ethnic mobilization (cf. Connor, 1984; Rockett, 1981).

2. Duncan (1982), Dunleavy (1981), and Miliband (1982) provide a discussion of the changing character of the capitalist state and a consideration of the significance of the ideology of liberal democracy from a marxist perspective. Miliband recognizes the contribution of this ideology to social stability thus: "So long as the achievement of a parliamentary majority appears possible, so long must any alternative strategy, based upon the expectation of a revolutionary seizure of power, remain of very marginal political significance" (1982, p. 157).

3. Plaid Cymru means the party of Wales. It is also referred to as the Blaid, employing a mutation in the initial consonant which occurs in Welsh and which is customarily used even when speaking or writing about the party in English.

2

Nationalist Uses of the Past

Nationalist ideology bases the legitimacy of the state on the unity deriving from a common national identity. Thus, the ruling elites of 'nation-states' have been concerned to bolster a sense of common nationality. Such concern was particularly acute in democratic polities as they extended the franchise to an increasingly larger segment of the population. As a consequence, the period of major polity democratization in Western European states, from the final decades of the nineteenth century up to the start of World War I, was also a period of great activity in building national awareness through the creation of national traditions. This process included enshrining national symbols, creating and embellishing national public ceremonial occasions, and building public monuments. The most fundamental way in which national traditions were created and communicated to the populace at large was through the encouragement of national histories and their communication via primary education, which was becoming compulsory during this period (Hobsbawm, 1983).

Minority nationalities faced two major obstacles in their attempts to develop similar bases for a national consciousness. In the first place, they were in direct competition with the alternative national identity propagated by the state, in virtually all of its manifestations, from choice of a national flag to interpretation of national history. Secondly, they possessed very few institutional resources to facilitate transmission of their own national symbols or national history to the populace at large. Educational institutions were state controlled, and the financial base and political influence required to stage elaborate national public ceremonies were generally unavailable.

In nineteenth-century Wales, the national elite were largely English-oriented in their careers and their status judgements, an orientation that was reinforced by their desire to participate fully in the opportunities and prestige associated with the expansion of the British empire. Thus, they wanted Welsh culture and history to present a favorable image when viewed from an English perspective. One result was a romanticized interpretation of Welsh history which emphasized the Welsh contribution to the consolidation of political power under the English monarchy. Under this interpretation, much was made of the Welsh ancestry of Henry Tudor: his victory at Bosworth Field in 1485, which secured for him the English crown, was depicted as the ascension of a descendant of the Welsh princes to rule over the ancient Brythonic realm of King Arthur. Another result of the English orientation of the Welsh national elite was their enshrinement of the Welsh rural folk tradition (P. Morgan, 1972; also cf. P. Morgan, 1983), emphasizing its antiquarian interest, and this at a time when increasing numbers of Welsh people were being absorbed into a new industrial working class serving the developing iron and coal industries in the southeastern valleys.

Thus, the nineteenth-century Welsh elite, for the most part, perceived the Welsh historical experience as, at best, contributory to the development of mainstream English national history.[1] However, their activities in another area, that of the establishment of national institutions for Wales, and in particular of a national university, provided the framework from which an alternative interpretation of Welsh history eventually emerged. Welsh colleges, established in the 1870s and 1880s in north, south, and mid Wales,[2] had begun to provide career opportunities for Welsh scholars in which success was less closely tied to English institutions and culture than formerly. When these colleges were brought together to create the federal University of Wales in 1893, the Welsh emphasis in research and teaching was further strengthened (K. O. Morgan, 1982, pp. 106–111).

The career of John Edward Lloyd, who studied at University College, Aberystwyth, and spent most of his professional career at the University College of North Wales at Bangor, initially as lecturer in history, eventually as department chairman, exemplified the importance of the Welsh colleges in the development of a national focus for Welsh historical studies. His book, *A History of Wales from the Earliest Times to the Edwardian Conquest*, published in 1911, was a seminal work in establishing Welsh history as a recognized field of study. While meeting standards of scholarly objectivity, the work was in the genre of national histories in its tone as well as its focus. It showed Llywelyn the Great to be an able and heroic leader in resisting the Anglo-Norman invaders, while the death, in 1282, of Llywelyn II, the last Prince of Wales, which ensured final victory for the conquest by Edward I, was seen as a tragedy for the Welsh nation (K. O. Morgan, 1982, pp. 102–103; J. F. Rees, 1963, pp. 36–37).

Given this intellectual foundation along with continued support by Welsh academic institutions, successive scholars produced a body of writings on Welsh history over the next several decades. These studies concentrated on medieval history, that is, on the history of the Welsh nation prior to its absorption by England under the Tudor monarchs. It was not until after 1945 that another generation of historians, responding to an altered concept of the bases of national identity, began to study more recent Welsh history.

While creating a national history was essentially an elite activity, the fruit of such intellectual researches had to be communicated to a wider public for it to reinforce national consciousness. Nationalists had few institutional resources available to them through which they could pursue this goal. Nevertheless, one institution, the National Eisteddfod, while not closely associated with the academic study of Welsh history, did stimulate interest in the Welsh past, both genuine and mythical. Eisteddfodau—cultural gatherings which featured poetic and musical competitions—were not new to Wales, even in the nineteenth century; the first recorded eisteddfod had been held in 1176. However, the annual National Eisteddfod was firmly established and given official standing in the latter part of the nineteenth century by the London Welsh working through their Cymmrodorion Society (Jenkins & Ramage, 1951). Their concern to improve education in Wales prompted them to sponsor a series of scholarly papers as part of the Eisteddfod's proceedings. They also brought to full flower the rituals and mystic imagery of the Gorsedd of Bards (the bardic court). While supposedly handed down from the ancient Druids, the Gorsedd was actually the invention of Iolo Morgannwg (Edward Williams, 1747–1826), a poet and mystic, who developed his ideas at the end of the eighteenth century. Although the bogus origins of the costumes and ritual were subsequently revealed, the success of the Eisteddfod as a national symbol and forum in a sense legitimized the symbolism on which its ceremonies relied (P. Morgan, 1983, pp. 56–62, 92). Its strength was further attested by its ability to evolve with the national movement. In the late nineteenth century, papers in the formal sessions, as well as general conversation on the Eisteddfod field, were overwhelmingly in English, and this at a time when Wales was almost entirely Welsh speaking (Edwards, 1976, p. 79; Jenkins & Ramage, 1951, p. 201). By the mid-twentieth century, however, the emphasis in the Eisteddfod had shifted to its role in strengthening the Welsh language and, in 1950, an all-Welsh rule was introduced to govern its competitions and all official activity. Within a few years, this rule had transformed the Eisteddfod into a bastion for the defense of the Welsh language.

The success of the Eisteddfod in communicating national values and embodying national sentiment was not matched in other areas. Little progress was made in introducing Welsh history into the schools, which remained under the control of the British educational establishment. Early in the twentieth century, an attempt to inaugurate such a program had been made by Owen M. Edwards, who, as Chief Inspector of Schools for Wales, pressed for greater inclusion of Welsh historical and cultural studies in the curriculum. While Edwards had some success in this regard, state control of school syllabi and examinations meant that Welsh history, if taught at all, remained an adjunct to the main history curriculum, which traced the rise and consolidation of the English state.

The continued inability of nationalists, into the second half of the twentieth century, fundamentally to influence the school curriculum meant that dependence on historic national identity as a basis for political mobilization was unlikely to prove successful. Nevertheless, with a few exceptions, this was a major theme of nationalist electoral messages well into the 1960s. It was an orientation that reflected the background and motivation of the majority of the leaders in the political nationalist movement. Indeed, a number of prominent early members of the Welsh Nationalist Party were themselves contributors to the body of writings on Welsh history. The party's founders had taken the historical existence of the Welsh nation as a primary argument for the establishment of separate Welsh political institutions. This argument proved persuasive only for a relatively small number of individuals who subsequently became party activists. It was much less compelling as a means of convincing voters to support nationalist candidates at elections. Thus, during the 1960s, Plaid Cymru shifted its emphasis to other arguments and issues, a move that was part of a general politicization of the party.[3] Following the defeat, in a popular referendum, of the Labour government's proposal for a Welsh Assembly, and the decline in the Blaid's vote in the 1979 general election, some party members began to advocate a return to the basic nationalist issue of self-government, with a greater emphasis on creating an active cadre of nationalists rather than attracting the tactical voter. Nevertheless, in spite of considerable soul-searching within the party during this period, few party leaders considered a reversion to its earlier, politically naive electoral style to be a serious option.

Plaid Cymru's experience suggested that while the development of a national history served both as an inspiration for some activists and as a basis for a national identity at variance with that propagated by the state, it could not be directly employed for political mobilization. The primary way in which national history could strengthen national consciousness was through its inclusion in school curricula, but efforts to secure the incorporation of Welsh history, in any other than a secondary role, into the British educational system failed.

WELSH HISTORY: ALTERNATIVE INTERPRETATIONS

The national history of a 'nation-state' chronicles the events through which a central political apparatus developed to become dominant over a particular territory. Since the process of state formation normally entailed absorption of outlying, culturally distinct regions by an expanding core, the histories of these other groups become a part of the narrative as they impinge upon the state-building process. Thus, British history inevitably became the history of the expansion of the English state and its assumption of power over the other peoples of the British Isles. Events in Ireland, Scotland, and Wales were selected and interpreted according to their effect upon this central theme (cf. Trevelyan, 1926, p. vii). Typically, in his two-volume history of the British Commonwealth, Ramsay Muir noted that "the bulk of the space is necessarily devoted to the history of England, because it was in England that the institutions and ideas characteristic of the whole Commonwealth had their birth and early development" (1927, p. v).

Such an orientation produced an impression of Welsh history fundamentally at variance with that created by a national history of Wales. A selection of works of British history illuminates the differences, in tone, in selection of important periods and events, and in interpretation of the significance of even the same events, between the history of Wales as a part of Britain and the history of Wales as a nation. In his discussion of the Roman conquest of Britain, for example, Trevelyan referred to the Welsh mountains as "reservoirs of savagery" from which "warlike tribes" emerged "to plunder the demilitarized inhabitants of city and villa in the plains below" (1926, p. 20). Other English historians emphasized the superficiality of the Roman influence in Britain (e.g., Sanderson, 1893, p. 19), pointing to the loss of Christianity after the barbarian invasions began and the existence of only "a few Roman words still surviving in the language of the Celtic-speaking Britons" (Tout, 1923, p. 15). Welsh historians, on the other hand, saw the legacy of the Roman conquest of Britain in the substantial influence of Latin on the Welsh language as well as in the introduction of Christianity to Wales and the subsequent development of the Celtic Church, both indications that Welsh contact with the Romans went well beyond military engagement (cf. Carter, 1966; Hardinge, 1972; Houlder, 1975; McNeill, 1974).

Many descriptions by English historians of the Anglo-Saxon invasions, following the withdrawal of the Romans, depicted the Celtic tribes as having been driven out of the English lowlands into the mountains of Wales (e.g., Sanderson, 1893, p. 26; Tout, 1923, p. 20; Trevelyan, 1926, pp. 42–44). This interpretation was refuted by Welsh historians who pointed to the known occupation of Wales by Celts since before the Roman era (cf. D. G.Jones, 1973a, p. 33). They argued that the Celts in England were largely absorbed by the invaders, rather than being driven en masse westward, and thus that the Welsh people of modern times occupied the same territory as did their Celtic forbears.

This period of Anglo-Saxon incursions received opposite interpretations by the two historical traditions. The centuries following the departure of the Romans, from a Welsh perspective, was a golden 'Age of the Saints' that saw the growth of the Welsh Church (Bowen, 1959) and a flowering of bardic poetry (Jackson, 1959; J. E. C. Williams, 1959). English historians viewed this same period as a 'Dark Age' and gave it scant attention, moving quickly to Augustine's arrival in the sixth century and the conversion of the Anglo-Saxons to Christianity. Macauley brought his summary of these centuries to a close with the observation that "at length the darkness begins to break; and the country which had been lost to view as Britain reappears as England" (1913, p. 5). Trevelyan described the period in somewhat more detail, but with scarcely more sensitivity to Welsh history, as follows:

It is ... difficult to exaggerate the injury done to Romano-British civilization. It was crushed out between two barbarisms—invading Saxondom and the Celtic revival. For the lowland districts where it had flourished were exactly the districts swept by the besom of the Saxon destroyer. In the Welsh mountains and on the Cornish moors the civilized refugees, deprived of their cities and estates and surrounded by brother-Celts far less civilized than themselves, forgot in a generation or two the arts and traditions that had once enabled them to look down on the Saxon brute. ... Surviving Celt and incoming Saxon alike were rude barbarians. Yet because the Saxon now lived in the lowlands, he began to evolve a civilization of his own, which was very soon superior to that of the Welsh mountaineers. [1926, p. 42]

A major theme in British history was the distinction made between tribal Wales and feudal England, with eventual English dominance explained by the evolution of a superior form of government. Trevelyan attributed the roots of this avowed superiority to the schism, lasting nearly two centuries, until 777, between the Church of Rome and the Celtic Church, following its rejection of Augustine's conditions for cooperation in conversion of the Anglo-Saxons.

The early adhesion of all the English Kingdoms to the Roman system of religion gave a great impetus to the movement towards racial unity, kingly and feudal power, systematic administration, legislation and taxation, and territorial as against tribal politics. The English, as we have seen, were already moving away from tribalism much more rapidly than the Celts. ... [1926, pp. 61–62]

Welsh historians interpreted the significance of the Welsh rejection of Augustine's conditions rather differently as representing the refusal of Welsh Christians "to place themselves under the direct control of Rome through a bishop established at Canterbury under a Saxon king" (Fenn, 1976, p. 7).

While not all English historians traced the distinction between English feudalism and Welsh tribalism to such an early period, they generally regarded it as the fundamental difference between the two countries during the early middle ages (cf. Barrow, 1956, pp. 211–213).

It is not necessary to say so much about the other three nations of the islands as we have said about England ... mainly because they were all three in a much more backward state than England. England, as we have seen, was organised upon a feudal basis... In the greater part of Wales, Scotland and Ireland the outstanding feature of the people's life was the survival of a tribal system, wherein power rested with hereditary chieftains, constantly at war with one another. [Muir, 1927, p. 77]

The validity of this distinction, particularly as an explanation of eventual English military dominance, was challenged by Welsh historians in their descriptions of the kingdoms established by strong Welsh leaders in the period prior to the Norman invasion of England in 1066. They pointed to Rhodri Mawr, who, in the ninth century, ruled Gwynedd, Seisyllwg, and Powys, thus controlling northwest, west, and mid-Wales. In the tenth century, his grandson, Hywel Dda, made himself ruler of the whole of Wales except for the southeast and became further renowned for his codification of Welsh law (Chadwick, 1959; G. Roberts, 1959b).

Whereas the Norman conquest of England in 1066 was a watershed in English history, this date had less significance to Welsh historians, who saw the Welsh resistance to the Anglo-Normans as a continuation of their struggles against the Anglo-Saxons. The Norman kings attempted to subdue Wales by granting lands in Wales "beyond the march" to military leaders who were expected to wrest control from the native Welsh princes. English historians generally depicted the Norman invaders of Wales as bearers of a higher civilization (cf. Fisher, 1936, p. 309). According to Trevelyan, these Marcher Lords,

represented a type of government more backward than that of England but more advanced than that of tribal Wales. ... To the tribal Celts the civilization forcibly imported by the Marcher Lords meant progress. [1926, pp. 209–210]

To Welsh historians, this period of resistance to the Marcher Lords represented the high point of Welsh national unity. Following the death of Henry I in 1135, a series of Welsh princes led a sustained rebellion against the Marcher Lords, achieving increased independence from England and increased Welsh unity. Llywelyn the Great, one of the ablest of the Welsh princes, effectively challenged the Anglo-Normans and, by the time of his death in 1240, had established his rule over most of Wales from his stronghold in Gwynedd in northwest Wales. After a brief period of disunity, his grandson Llywelyn II reestablished control over an area even greater than that ruled by Llywelyn the Great at the height of his power. By 1258, Wales had attained virtually complete sovereignty (I. L. Foster, 1959; Pierce, 1959). The major break in Welsh history came when this period of Welsh sovereignty was ended by the English invasion under Edward I and the resulting death, in 1282, of Llywelyn II, the last Welsh Prince of Wales (G. Roberts, 1959a).

English historians had a very different perspective on the two Llywelyns and the conquest by Edward I. One characterized the appellation 'the Great,' given to Llywelyn I, as "the greatness of a 'might-have-been'" but conceded it was justified by "his political sagacity, a rare quality among the Welsh of his day, and one not inherited by his more brilliant and ambitious grandson" (Barrow, 1956, p. 221). Many blamed Llywelyn II for bringing the English invasion on himself (cf. Barrow, 1956, pp. 349–357).

Llewelyn had been treated with great forbearance. Again and again his evasions had been met with a further summons but no hostile movement. ... War was deliberately provoked by the Welsh leader: he had placed himself in the position of a rebel, whom his overlord could justly punish by the confiscation of his estates. [Vickers, 1914, pp. 19–20]

For most of the generation of Welsh historians inspired by J. E. Lloyd, Welsh national history came to an end with the death of Llywelyn II. A few saw it continuing through the career of Owain Glyndwr, who led an uprising early in the fifteenth century that resulted in several years of Welsh sovereignty. However, virtually all regarded the Act of Union in 1536 as marking the end of a distinctive Welsh national history. This Act incorporated Wales into the English administrative and political system, proscribing the use of the Welsh language in any official capacity and eliminating nearly all separate Welsh organizations[4] (D. Williams, 1950). What these Welsh historians regarded as the end of Welsh national history, English historians, often claiming that the Welsh ancestry of Henry VIII helped to reconcile the two nations (Fisher, 1936, p. 309; Muir, 1927, p. 112; Tout, 1923, pp. 350–351), depicted as of undoubted benefit to Wales and an act of high statesmanship (cf. Elton, 1955, p. 198). "Henry VIII . . .

understood Wales and solved its problems by a policy which combined repression of disorder with justice to the Celtic population" (Trevelyan, 1926, p. 359).

In the decades following World War II, some Welsh historians began to investigate more recent Welsh history and, in the process, extended the definition of what constituted a national history for Wales. Since Wales was no longer definable in terms of autonomous political institutions, their investigations redefined the bases for studying Wales as a unit. Initially, they focussed on the nineteenth-century nationalist movement, interpreted in its broadest sense as both a cultural and political awakening of national consciousness (cf. K. O. Morgan, 1963, pp. v–ix). In particular, they emphasized the distinctiveness of Welsh politics within the British political system, subsequent to electoral reform and the establishment of Liberal Party hegemony in Wales. This distinctiveness persisted into the twentieth century as Welsh politics was transformed by the growth of the labor movement and the gradual assumption of political power by the Labour Party. Many Welsh historians turned to the study of working-class history to uncover the bases of Welsh national consciousness (e.g., G. Williams, 1966), and an historical journal, *Llafur*, which dealt specifically with the Welsh working class, was established in 1972.

Nevertheless, the treatment of Wales as a national unit in historical investigations remained a matter of dispute, given its lack of political institutions, and several Welsh historians produced works in which they wrestled with the problem of the source of such unity and the justification for such an historical focus (e.g., D. Smith, 1984; G. A. Williams, 1985). The justification for treating Wales as an entity with its own national history, in fact, owed much to the revival of the nationalist movement in the 1960s. However, the influence was not all in a single direction. The relationship of the political nationalist movement to Welsh history had been close from its inception, and some fundamental changes in the movement, in particular its gradual adoption of a more socialist position,[5] were bolstered if not wholly inspired by these new directions in the writing of Welsh history.

NATIONAL HISTORY AND NATIONALIST POLITICS

The emphasis of the Welsh Nationalist Party in the pre–World War II period was on the preservation and encouragement of Welsh culture, and its nationalist message relied heavily on Wales's historic identity as a nation. Many prominent party members, among them Saunders Lewis, G. J. Williams, and Ambrose Bebb, contributed, through their own writings, to the development of a Welsh national history (P. Morgan, 1972, p. 39). And they used this history to justify the nationalist position. In his seminal speech on the principles of nationalism, given at the first of the Welsh Nationalist Party's annual summer schools in 1926, Saunders Lewis argued that the concept of nationalism stemming from the era of European state formation was materialist and hence unjustifiable. Welsh nationalism should seek its roots in a much older nationalist principle, that of the early Middle Ages, when respect for a diversity of cultures was combined with an acceptance of the international moral authority of the Christian Church (S. Lewis, 1975, p. 9).

Lewis, who was president of the party from 1926 to 1939, was himself involved professionally in the recovery and reinterpretation of Welsh history. His book on the history of Welsh literature to 1535, which was published in 1932, was described by a fellow nationalist as "a kind of blueprint for his creation of a new nation in Wales, based on her worthy past" (D. J. Williams, 1973, p. 4). He believed that bringing an awareness of Wales's historic nationhood to the people of Wales was a major mission for the nationalist party and would produce increased popular support (D. H. Davies, 1983, p. 184). This approach continued to influence thinking in the party and provided an important focus of nationalist activity into the 1960s. In its 1946 summer school, for example, Plaid Cymru organized a symposium on "The Historical Bases of Welsh Nationalism."[6] In addition, numerous party publications, including several short historical treatises,[7] attested to the efficacy of Welsh history to convince people of the rightness of the nationalist cause. Typical of these was a 1949 pamphlet stating, "Our main task is a spiritual one. It is to restore a sense of Welsh nationhood, a feeling of pride in our own people, a pride in the greatness of our heritage . . ." (D. M. Lloyd, 1949). This belief was echoed as late as 1961 in another party publication which contended, "One of Plaid Cymru's most important tasks is to put the people of Wales in touch with their own past, make them more sure of their identity . . ." (I. B. Rees, 1975, p. 11).

Gwynfor Evans, who was president of Plaid Cymru from 1945 to 1981, and Member of Parliament for Carmarthen from 1966 to 1970 and 1974 to 1979, was an exponent of this philosophy and relied upon it extensively in his electioneering. He regularly spoke on the early history of Wales at political gatherings and drew lessons from it for contemporary Wales. His opening remarks in a speech before the House of Commons made during an early debate on devolution provided an example of this oratorical style.

The Bill would not be before the House but for the growth of Scottish and Welsh national consciousness. I hope that hon. Members realise that they are dealing with two nations, two of the oldest in Europe. About three and a half centuries ago, in a play performed before the Council of Wales, John Milton wrote of Wales that she was an "ancient nation, proud in arms." At that time, the magnificent literature of Wales had an unbroken history of a thousand years. Welsh was the language of government and the law in Wales when French was the language of government and the law here. The House is dealing not with two regions, two parts of the country, two colonies, but with two old national communities. [Great Britain, 1976, p. 1]

Evans published a popular history of Wales, in both Welsh and English versions, in the early 1970s.[8] This book built upon the preceding decades of Welsh historical research but departed from this tradition in its explicitly nationalist perspective. It was interspersed with lessons drawn from early Welsh history and applied to contemporary Wales. For example, in considering the diminution of Welsh national consciousness following the Tudor ascension, Evans observed that "the tragic mistake of the Welsh ... was to aim at government by a Welshman in London instead of a Welsh government in Wales" (1974, p. 277). The book itself was published after Plaid Cymru had moved away from the explicit use of the history of Wales as a justification for nationalist ideology and dependence upon its propagation as a primary means of creating nationalists. Nevertheless, it provided the most fully developed example of the ways in which national history was used by Welsh nationalists prior to the 1960s: first, to justify nationalist ideology, in particular the belief in the need for Welsh political institutions to safeguard Welsh culture; and, second, to bolster a sense of Welsh identity and thereby win converts to political nationalism.

Awareness of a separate Welsh historical tradition did lead some individuals to political nationalism. When, in 1976 and 1977, a cross-section of some fifty Plaid Cymru members were asked the reasons for their becoming nationalists, 20 percent mentioned an academic experience that created such awareness. Several had been inspired by a teacher who encouraged an appreciation of their Welsh heritage. Others recounted a more negative experience of becoming aware of the inferior role granted to Wales in British history. One individual developed a conscious sense of Welsh, as apart from British, identity at about school-leaving age, when, while studying for accountancy examinations, he came across phrases like "according to the laws of England, which includes Wales" (interview, 4 October 1976). Another recalled,

I was always very aware of being Welsh and not English and was forever searching for mention of the Welsh in history books. I remember being under the impression that the pictures always showed the English on horses with the Welsh standing in the mud down below. [Interview, 4 April 1977]

Only one individual said he had been converted to nationalism as a direct result of a school history course, without having had any prior sense of Welsh identity at all. This person came from an English-speaking area and said his parents had no consciousness of Welsh identity. However, his secondary school headmaster, following recommendations of the Welsh Joint Education Committee, gave prominence to the history of Wales in the modern European history course. This individual became a nationalist and joined Plaid Cymru while still a schoolboy due to the influence of this course.

However, Plaid Cymru's emphasis over several decades on educating the people of Wales in their country's history produced few active nationalists and no popular electoral support. Their educational efforts were limited by the very small number of active party members as well as by their lack of control over established channels of communication, in particular the schools. In the 1960s, Plaid Cymru abandoned this emphasis, as it was transformed from a diffuse national movement into a political party intent on winning elections, not simply fighting them for symbolic or educational purposes. One representative of that element in the Blaid responsible for effecting this transformation stated that those who had controlled the party executive from World War II through the 1950s had no clear immediate political objectives but just wanted "to revive Hywel Dda and Llywelyn Fawr for the twentieth century" (interview, 18 May 1977).

While nationalists continued to accept the importance of Welsh history in building a self-conscious national identity, few any longer perceived Plaid Cymru's mission as one primarily of bringing such a national historical consciousness to the people of Wales directly. In interviews with nineteen of the twenty-four prospective parliamentary candidates who had been adopted by Plaid Cymru in the spring of 1977, only one argued for the need "to educate people about nationalism" even though "there is no hope of winning" (interview, 23 May 1977). Another, when asked about probable issues in a parliamentary campaign, said, "There is the basic nationalist issue of self-government. This really is not an issue in people's minds, but I will plug it since part of the reason for standing is missionary work" (interview, 30 May 1977).

These two candidates alone described their primary goal as educating the people in order to restore their consciousness of being Welsh. Other candidates also spoke of educating the electorate, a reason often given for contesting a seat where the possibility of victory was slight. However, such education was meant to inform the voters of Plaid Cymru's improved political status by presenting its positions on specific issues. The prospective parliamentary candidate in Pembroke, an area where Plaid Cymru had a very poor electoral history, described his approach, which was new to the constituency:

You have to show your concern with social and economic issues before people will accept the cultural argument. For example, we have developed a strong association with civic leaders in Fishguard to try to stop British Rail from closing the link to Ireland. This impresses people with the social and community responsibility of Plaid Cymru and shows that we are not just culture enthusiasts. [Interview, 29 May 1977]

A candidate in one of the valley constituencies said that his branch had found it "had to work at the local level to reduce our image of being fanatics" (interview, 19 May 1977). Another, who did not reside in his rural border constituency, stressed his frequent visits and his involvement with the everyday concerns of constituents. "If I can help people with ordinary problems, like complaints about garbage or a bill or that sort of thing, then they will trust me with bigger issues like the language, which are really more important to me personally" (interview, 14 December 1976). And the candidate for a constituency in an industrial area of northeast Wales recalled that observations he made during the 1972 by-election in Merthyr Tydfil convinced him of the importance of winning seats on local councils to improve the party's chances in parliamentary elections.

In the Merthyr by-election, Plaid Cymru had the better candidate, a better campaign, and we worked harder. But on polling day there was a local Labour councillor at every polling booth greeting people as they came in. People remember something he may have done for them, their conscience pricks them for one reason or another, and they end up voting Labour again like they have done all their lives instead of taking the plunge of switching to Plaid Cymru. [Interview, 4 June 1977]

Another reason for the decreasing use of appeals based on Wales's historic national identity was the nature of the constituency nationalists had been trying harder to attract since the early 1960s. As Plaid Cymru began to aspire to conventional political power, the party had to recognize that the center of such power in Wales lay in the southeast, particularly in the populous county of Mid Glamorgan, where 20 percent of the total population of Wales reside. There, the electorate was, for the most part, non-Welsh speaking and politically sophisticated, with a long tradition of trade-union organization. In spite of having little popular awareness of Welsh national history, voters were strongly Welsh in their self-identity. One parliamentary candiate in a valley constituency, himself a Welsh speaker and product of a traditional Welsh nonconformist background, expressed his and the party's acceptance of this non-traditional Welsh identity:

I believe that there is a non-Welsh-speaking yet distinctively Welsh culture and that this is what is to be found in Ebbw Vale. . . . For a long time Plaid Cymru did not seem to care about the valleys or their problems at all but that has changed now and it is Labour that does not care. [Interview, 23 March 1977]

For these reasons, most party leaders felt it was both patronizing and counter-productive to campaign in the valleys by stressing the restoration of Welsh historic identity. Rather, they assumed that a consciousness of being Welsh already existed there and campaigned on economic and social issues of more immediate relevance to the Welsh working-class constituency they were addressing. They might state that ultimately self-government was the only solution for Welsh problems, but such a conclusion was not the centerpiece of campaign rhetoric.

I believe that the best approach to adopt to the workers is to stress the need for Wales to be planned as a unit which only its own institutions can do properly, and this will bring economic development. Then you can also bring in the dream of nationhood and what it means. But you cannot argue the converse. [Interview, 23 March 1977]

The Blaid's success in becoming an accepted, if marginal, participant in the British electoral process raised fears among some activists that the party was in danger of being absorbed into the system and of losing sight of its long-term nationalist objectives. An internal report on the status of the party following its setbacks in 1979 asserted that "the party as a whole ... appears to be agreed that we have become too much of a respectable, mainstream political party and too preoccupied with fighting elections and with Westminster-based consensus and compromise politics" (Plaid Cymru, 1981b, p. 4). Working to revive national consciousness through the use of Welsh history was one area into which the report suggested redirecting members' energies.

One of the main factors undermining the feeling of nationhood and Welsh identity is ignorance of Welsh history which receives such scant attention in our schools. We must press for an increase in Welsh history teaching and at the same time the party can play a more direct role by encouraging the discussion of Welsh history at meetings of canghennau [local branches] and at such national events as the summer school. [Plaid Cymru, 1981b, p. 11]

In fact, several other areas proved far more fruitful than that of developing national identity through fostering the study of Welsh history. The utility of national history for a nationalist movement, beyond inspiring a few individuals to an active nationalist commitment, can be realized only if control over the educational system can be achieved. Welsh history did not prove itself an effective weapon for winning such control. Far more useful in this regard was the Welsh language whose crucial role in the nationalist movement may now be examined.

NOTES

1. The concept of a Welsh nation, which had had its own separate history until the narrative was broken by its conquest by England, can be found in the writings of Michael D. Jones (1822–1898) and Emrys ap Iwan (Robert Ambrose Jones, 1851–1906). However, neither man produced a formal national history of Wales. Michael D. Jones was an early champion of the right of the Welsh nation to its own political institutions. He attempted to provide a Welsh state by founding a Welsh colony in Patagonia (Argentina). He was a major influence on many of the young Welsh radicals of the 1880s, in particular Lloyd George and T. E. Ellis (K. O. Morgan, 1963, pp. 19, 58). However, neither his ideas nor those of Emrys ap Iwan led to any real political appeal based on Welsh nationhood or to the formation of an independent political party, which both advocated (D. G. Jones, 1973a, p. 55).

2. The University College of Wales was established in Aberystwyth in 1872, the University College of South Wales and Monmouth in Cardiff in 1883, and the University College of North Wales in Bangor in 1884.

3. The style did not entirely disappear from Plaid Cymru electioneering. Gwynfor Evans, party president from 1945 to 1981, was noted for this type of campaign rhetoric.

4. Only two organizations remained to differentiate Wales from England. One, a distinct system of higher courts, namely, the Courts of the King's Great Sessions in Wales, included all the Welsh counties except Monmouth and survived until 1830. The second, the Council in the Marches of Wales, was abolished in 1689 (W. O. Williams, 1960). A recent revisionist history of the Tudor period in Wales by Glanmor Williams (1987) emphasizes the continuity in Welsh life throughout this period and downplays the extent to which the Act of Union was a major watershed in Welsh history and the main reason for the subsequent decline in Welsh culture. But see G. Evans (1988b) for a rebuttal of this reinterpretation.

5. See Chapter Four.

6. The lectures given at this symposium were published by Plaid Cymru in 1950 under the title *Seiliau Hanesyddol Cenedlaetholdeb Cymru* [The Historical Bases of Welsh Nationalism].

7. *The Welsh Tradition of Gwent* and *The Vale of Glamorgan, Its History and Traditions*, both of which were reprints of lectures given by Professor G. J. Williams (n.d.; 1972), and *The Welsh Condition* by Emyr Humphreys (n.d.).

8. *Aros Mae* was published in 1971 and *Land of My Fathers* in 1974.

3

Two Tongues, One Voice

Although political separatist movements are very commonly found among minority language groups, social theorists generally have rejected language as a causative element in ethnic political conflict (O'Barr & O'Barr, 1976). Nevertheless, the centrality of linguistic issues in so many minority nationalist movements suggests that the ethnic language makes substantive contributions to such movements and does not function solely as a mark of group identity (Fishman, 1972; Fishman, Gertner, Lowy, & Milan, 1985).

In Wales, the language movement became the most dynamic and arguably the most successful manifestation of Welsh nationalism in the twentieth century. Furthermore, in spite of the internal political conflicts that can grow from, or be aggravated by, a linguistically divided population (see Figure 3.1), the language movement, on balance, has enhanced Welsh unity and strengthened the political nationalist movement. [See Bowen and Carter (1975) for a more detailed analysis of the geographical distribution of the Welsh language in 1971.]

No simple linear relationship exists between the numerical strength of a language and its utility to a political movement. While Welsh speakers greatly increased in number during the nineteenth century, the language was not used as a basis for political mobilization. Both local and national Welsh elites regarded it either as a handicap to be overcome or as of primarily antiquarian interest. It was in the twentieth century that Welsh attained political saliency, in spite of the decline in the numbers of Welsh speakers (see Table 3.1).

Figure 3.1
Distribution of the Welsh Language in 1971, by County

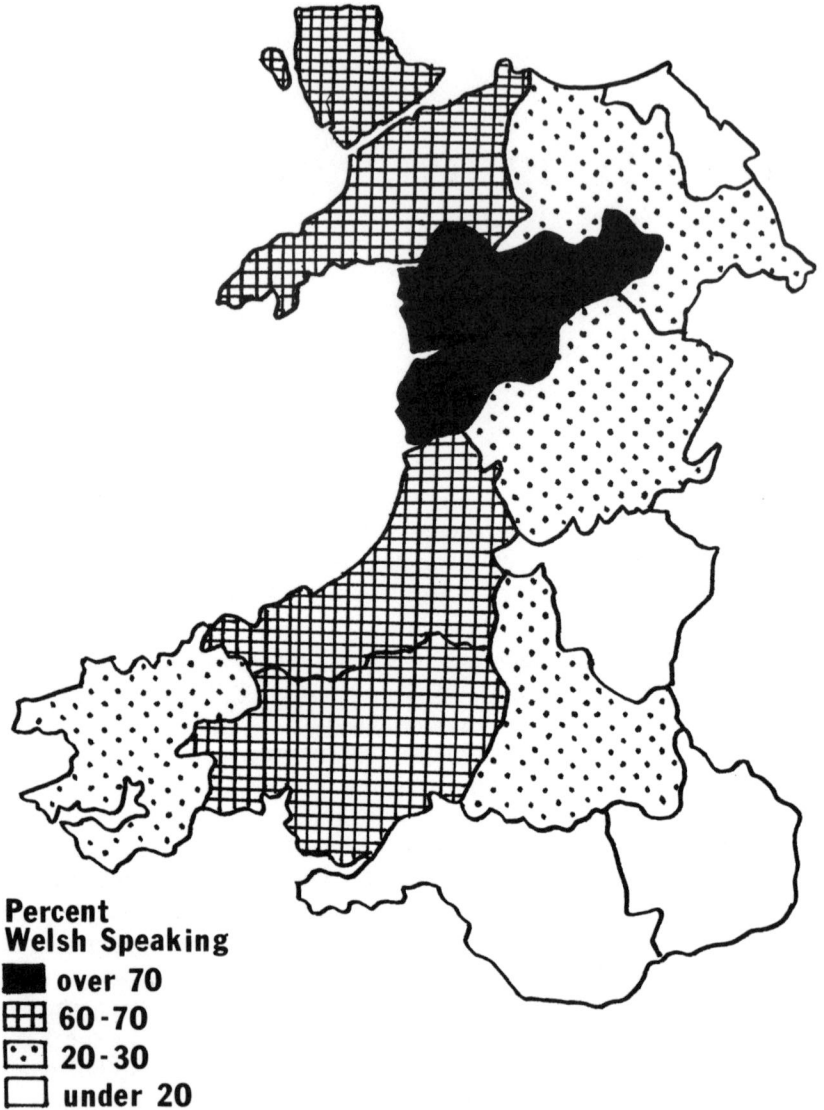

The increased political importance of minority languages over the past two centuries (Deutsch, 1942; Das Gupta, 1970) was a consequence of the growth in the power of the state. As the state began to interfere more frequently and more directly in the everyday lives of ordinary people, the administrative pressure to standardize its dealings with the populace increased. One way in which state elites commonly pursued such uniformity was through the elimination of minority languages. Ethnic elites were often coopted into facilitating the erosion of their own language if there were positions in the state power structure open to them.

This was essentially what happened in Wales in the nineteenth century. The Welsh elite, a large proportion of whom were London-based, were concerned with using their positions as leaders of Welsh society to win approbation and influence in English society. Of major importance in conditioning their essentially English orientation was their desire to participate in the opportunities and prestige associated with the growth of the empire. Thus, they did not seek to use the Welsh language as a political weapon against the system that sustained them. Nor did they make any serious effort to protect the language against English incursions, although the threat to the survival of Welsh began to be apparent toward the end of the century. The use they made of the Welsh language, to argue for special educational measures for Wales, was ultimately to prove harmful to the cause of language maintenance. Aside from this, they largely confined their interest in the language to promoting its study as a romantic and rather esoteric pursuit.

As the ravages of state linguistic policies became more apparent in Wales, and in Ireland and Scotland as well, individuals whose social

Table 3.1
Welsh Speakers in Wales, 1901–1981

Year	Number in Thousands	Percent
1901	930	50
1911	977	44
1921	922	37
1931	909	29
1951	714	29
1961	656	26
1971	542	21
1981	520	19

Source: Great Britain (1975a), p. 48.

positions encouraged a degree of intellectual independence and whose vocations entailed commitment to their national language began to resist the process of linguistic assimilation. The Welsh language was the main inspiration for the coalescence of the small nationalist cadre who were the founders of the Welsh Nationalist Party (later called Plaid Cymru).[1] These individuals were, for the most part, intellectuals, academic and religious leaders, and literary figures, rather than politicians. Their lack of political experience mitigated against the movement's achieving any early political success. However, their concern for the survival of the language, based as it was on its central role in their professional and personal lives, ensured a steadfast and dedicated leadership core, unlikely to desert the movement out of political self-interest. A central tenet of the nationalist ideology they propounded was that the problem of linguistic and cultural decline resulted from political rule by an external power. Although their argument also linked cultural oppression to economic disadvantage, nationalists had little success in broadening their appeal. They were relatively powerless in the face of external forces, both formal state policies and state-supported economic arrangements, that were forcing the majority of the populace to abandon their language and attempt to assimilate into the dominant English culture.

However, with the growth of the welfare society after World War II, the relationship of the state with minority groups and minority languages became more complex. As the state elite attempted to improve social justice and social welfare, they also provided, quite unwittingly, opportunities for Welsh-language supporters to take positive action to aid their cause. Plaid Cymru, committed as it was to seeking a solution for the language problem through political campaigning, did not assume the lead in this postwar language movement. Instead two other nationalist groupings developed: one was composed mainly of university students, who relied on civil disobedience in their campaign to secure official recognition for the Welsh language; the second, initially led by a Welsh-speaking professional class but quickly winning support from non–Welsh-speaking, working-class parents, employed pressure-group tactics to establish Welsh-medium schools in what had been, since 1870, a completely English educational system.

Guaranteeing the right to use Welsh in official contexts became more important as communication between individuals and the bureaucracy increased under the new welfare programs. Language activists campaigned vigorously and, in 1967, obtained official legal recognition for the language through the Welsh Language Act. This proved to be the first success in a continuing campaign of nonviolent direct action that later saw the provision of road signs and government forms in Welsh, as well as the achievement of the right to correspond with the bureaucracy in Welsh and enhanced status for the language in courts of law.

The significance for the nationalist movement of the campaign for Welsh-medium education went beyond the establishment of Welsh-medium schools. It contributed as well to the establishment of special bureaucratic structures for Wales as a whole. The use of a distinctive language in the schools provided a convincing argument for special educational arrangements of all sorts. Thus, the Welsh language provided an essential rationale for the growth of a Welsh infrastructure within the bureaucracy and, as such, it fostered administrative unity for the whole of Wales.

During the 1960s and 1970s, Plaid Cymru, as the political arm of the nationalist movement, concentrated on establishing its political respectability and avoided active campaigning on the language. The party benefitted from the strengthening of Welsh identity that derived from the language movement, but it feared the potential divisiveness of the language issue. However, following the demoralizing political losses of 1979, both in the referendum on the Labour government's proposed Welsh Assembly and in the general election, Plaid Cymru turned to the still-strong language movement as a way of rebuilding morale. For the first time, the party took the lead in what was the final stage of a major language campaign to establish a Welsh television channel.

THE WELSH LANGUAGE AND PLAID CYMRU

The most striking difference between the founders of the Welsh Nationalist Party and the nationalists of the nineteenth century was not their advocacy of Welsh home rule but the centrality they accorded to the Welsh language (D. H. Davies, 1983, p. 180). A majority of the founders and early party members were in professional positions: they were school teachers, ministers of religion, and college lecturers, rather than coal miners and quarrymen.[2] As teachers of Welsh language, literature, and history, or as interpreters of the Welsh nonconformist tradition, their main motivation for entering the unfamiliar world of politics was to ensure the retention and extension of the Welsh language. In his first major address to the new party in 1926, Saunders Lewis, the party's president for most of its first two decades, maintained that nationalism based on any principle other than linguistic and cultural survival was an essentially immoral concept. The single acceptable rationale behind the formation of a Welsh nationalist party was the belief that the Welsh language could flourish only if Wales had its own political institutions (S. Lewis, 1975; also cf. D. G. Jones, 1973a).

Given the centrality of the language in the nationalist ideology he propounded, it was not surprising that Saunders Lewis advocated, in the same 1926 lecture, that Welsh be made the only official language of Wales. The Welsh Nationalist Party's early stance on the language, while somewhat more cautious, reflected Lewis's attitudes quite closely. However, beginning about 1930, the party began to develop a more moderate position (D. H. Davies, 1983, p. 71). Initially, it had expressed on its membership forms that its intent was to make Welsh an official language and a medium of education. By 1932, however, the three essential objectives, to which all members were expected to subscribe, were formulated as: self-government for Wales; the preservation of Welsh culture, language, and traditions; and membership for Wales in the League of Nations[3] (Butt Philip, 1975, p. 16).

Nevertheless, Nationalist Party members were much more deeply committed to the cause of the language than that organization's relatively moderate official stance made apparent. The party itself was almost exclusively Welsh speaking, in its conferences and summer schools and in all internal communications, until after World War II. When publication of an English-language monthly paper was begun in 1932, under the prodding of a few individuals who recognized the necessity of bringing the nationalist message to non–Welsh-speaking Welshmen in the populous southeastern valleys, there was a great deal of resistance from within the ranks. Thus, in the decade from 1929 to 1939, while Nationalist Party publications projected an image of a bilingual movement (besides the English-language paper, approximately equal numbers of Welsh and English pamphlets were produced), the party itself was nearly totally Welsh speaking in internal organization and membership (D. H. Davies, 1983, pp. 179–186; also cf. J. E. Jones, 1970, pp. 82–84).

While party policy consistently advocated working through the electoral system to win self-government and thereby ensure the survival of the Welsh language, the predominantly middle-class, nonpolitical membership was reluctant to enter the political fray. Frustrated by inability to put up significant numbers of nationalist candidates in elections, Saunders Lewis determined to undertake a symbolic illegal act against the British state (D. H. Davies, 1983, pp. 153–160). The target chosen was a Royal Air Force bombing school, whose proposed establishment on the Lleyn Peninsula was regarded as certain to be detrimental to the language and culture of this completely Welsh-speaking area. On 8 September 1936, Lewis and two other party officials set fire to some workmen's huts on the base and then turned themselves over to the authorities (cf. Dafydd Jenkins, 1975). Their action and subsequent prison terms won them broad public support. However, this enthusiasm was short-lived; the only long-term benefits were some new members and the creation of an evocative nationalist myth.

And since Saunders Lewis had never intended that the action initiate a sustained campaign of civil disobedience, the party quickly returned to its nominal emphasis on the electoral process. It was further encouraged in this direction by the publicity Lewis's candidacy received in the 1942 by-election for the University of Wales parliamentary seat.

Events in the immediate postwar years stimulated further attempts to combat nationalism's image as being for Welsh speakers only. In this period, the state's assumption of new economic planning powers and the nationalization of basic industry created the potential means to build a unified Welsh economic base. Plaid Cymru leadership recognized the importance of securing Welsh administrative units in these various government economic schemes. Furthermore, an influx of new members, mostly returning servicemen, also pushed the party into more practical political activity. Thus, in the 1945 and 1946 by-election campaigns in three predominantly non–Welsh-speaking constituencies in the southeast, Plaid Cymru candidates made extensive use of English and emphasized economic rather than cultural issues. The party made a strong showing, although its favorable results were due in large part to special postwar circumstances.[4] However, the Blaid's gains in this period were transitory: the party failed to realize nationalist economic objectives, and its close inner network of Welsh-speaking, middle-class members resisted efforts to transform the party from a cultural organization, albeit one with a political agenda, into a genuine political party. The Welsh Republican Movement, formed in 1948 by a small group of ex-servicemen, was an attempt to break down this clublike atmosphere and alter the linguistic and cultural emphasis of the nationalist movement. The organization published an English-language paper for nearly a decade, but as a movement it was relatively inactive by the early 1950s. Most of its members moved into Plaid Cymru, where they tried to influence the nationalist image from within the party ranks, although a few, including the later Lord Gwilym Prys Davies, joined the Labour Party.

Plaid Cymru's next major reformulation of its language policy occurred in the 1960s, the decade which also brought its first significant electoral successes. During this period, increasing numbers of non-Welsh speakers joined the party, and the Blaid began to shed its Welsh-speakers-only image. Responding partly to these changes in party composition and partly to perceived requirements for electoral success, party leaders began to expound a policy of bilingualism, although the first official mention of a bilingual nation did not occur until 1969 (Butt Philip, 1975, p. 117).

During the decade and a half prior to the 1979 referendum and general election, Plaid Cymru concentrated on winning a measure of political respectability while other organizations took the lead in campaigns to defend the Welsh language. Most Plaid Cymru leaders, both Welsh- and non-Welsh speakers, came to view the language issue as a political liability, even though virtually all of them were personally very strong supporters of the Welsh language. The attitude of most candidates and workers was that the party's name as the only viable electoral choice for those who put the language high on their political priorities was unassailable, but that to stress the issue in their electioneering would only harm the party's prospects among less linguistically committed voters. This general attitude was characteristic of nationalists in both Welsh- and non–Welsh-speaking areas. Dafydd Elis Thomas, Plaid Cymru MP for Merioneth, a predominantly Welsh-speaking constituency in north Wales, who had himself been very active on behalf of the language, said that his successful 1974 parliamentary campaign "was deliberately geared to move us out of the cultural nationalist base. It was fought mainly on economic issues" (interview, 28 September 1976). In predominantly English-speaking areas, most candidates, interviewed in 1976 and 1977, claimed that the language was simply not a major issue and that the Blaid appeared heedless of other problems if it stressed the language at their expense. A few felt that if mishandled, so that people came to fear that they might be forced to learn Welsh to get or keep a job, the language issue could become a liability.[5]

The trend within Plaid Cymru in the 1960s and 1970s to deemphasize the linguistic and cultural aspects of nationalism did not amount to a rejection of the goal of Welsh-language maintenance and extension by nationalists themselves. Many party workers whose activities lay primarily in the conventional political sphere still cited the language as their main source of inspiration. As one prospective parliamentary candidate remarked, "Without the language the mainspring would go out of my motivation. Welsh freedom would still be worth working for, but I would not be as passionate about it" (interview, 30 May 1977). Another activist, whose work as a councillor in local government was primarily concerned with the mundane problems of community politics, analyzed his motivation in terms harking back to the rationalization for the Welsh nationalist movement originally advanced by Saunders Lewis.

There would not be much point in the nationalist movement if the language were lost since that is the main part of Welsh identity. The reason for advocating self-government is that a London government simply does not really perceive the problem of language maintenance. [Interview, 4 October 1976]

Thus, many of the individuals who participated in shifting the Blaid's tactical emphasis toward more conventional political issues still gave the language as the primary reason for their personal commitment to the nationalist movement. Their emphasis on conventional electoral politics was in agreement with the general plan for cultural and linguistic survival laid out by the party's founders. Furthermore, these cultural nationalists were in very similar professional and social positions to the founding members. And while they appeared readier to engage in practical politics than early party members had been, they were no more disposed to undertake other forms of political action. On the other hand, the new members, on which the Blaid's transformation in the 1960s was primarily based, professed to have joined the party out of socialist convictions and were not linguistic nationalists. A majority were non-Welsh speaking, and, although some eventually undertook to learn Welsh, their primary concern was that Plaid Cymru begin to challenge the hegemony of the Labour Party in south Wales. In this endeavour, they saw the language issue as irrelevant, if not detrimental. Thus, in spite of the language's central position in nationalist ideology and its importance to many party members, Plaid Cymru did not play a major role in the campaign which succeeded in achieving for Welsh both enhanced status and extended public use.

THE POLITICIZATION OF THE LANGUAGE ISSUE

By the beginning of the 1960s, disillusionment with constitutional methods had set in, particularly among younger members, as a result of disappointing election results and general lack of progress in securing any nationalist goals. Then, in February 1962, Saunders Lewis, who had retired from active political life in 1945, delivered a radio lecture which crystallized these doubts and offered a new direction for nationalist activity. In this lecture, he reversed his earlier position that only self-government could save the Welsh language:

In my opinion, if any kind of self-government for Wales were obtained before the Welsh language was acknowledged and used as an official language in local authority and state administration in the Welsh-speaking parts of our country, then the language would never achieve official status at all, and its demise would be quicker than it will be under English rule. [S. Lewis, 1973, p. 141]

He argued that the crisis facing the language was the only political issue to which the Welsh people should devote their energies, and he issued a call for direct action and civil disobedience to win official recognition for the Welsh language in Wales.

Although few realized it at the time, this speech was directed at Plaid Cymru in an effort to galvanize it into a different kind of activity from its, until then, futile electoral campaigning (C. Davies, 1973). It did not have this effect on the Blaid. However, at the Plaid Cymru summer school the following July, a group of youthful members established a new organization, Cymdeithas yr Iaith Gymraeg (the Welsh Language Society), dedicated to direct action to secure official recognition for the Welsh language. The society's first campaign was for Welsh court summonses and its first illegal act was a sit-down demonstration, in Feburary 1963, that blocked traffic on Trefechan Bridge leading into Aberystwyth, Dyfed.[6] Most of the demonstrators were students at the University College of Wales in Aberystwyth. The purpose of this demonstration was to elicit summonses which could then be refused for being in English. However, no arrests were made, and it was not until 1966 that a Cymdeithas member was first imprisoned for protesting the lack of motor vehicle tax forms in Welsh.[7] The campaign that produced the most publicity along with a very large number of arrests was the campaign for bilingual road signs. Initially activists concentrated on painting out English signs, later they began to remove them completely. This campaign, along with Cymdeithas yr Iaith's opposition to the Investiture of the Prince of Wales at Caernarfon Castle in 1969, elicited a great deal of unfavorable public reaction directed both at Cymdeithas yr Iaith and nationalism in general (C. Davies, 1973). Nevertheless, judged either by government response or by its overall impact on Welsh society, the bilingual signs campaign was one of the most successful Cymdeithas campaigns ever.

Prior to the growth of this form of language activism, decades of conventional political nationalism had had no impact on the pervasive official disregard of the Welsh language. To that point, the only significant legislation on the language in the twentieth century had been the 1942 Welsh Courts Act, which allowed Welsh speakers to give evidence in Welsh if they considered they were at a disadvantage using English. In 1963, shortly after the Trefechan Bridge demonstration, the government appointed a committee to inquire into the legal status of the language. This committee, known as the Hughes Parry Committee, reported in 1965, recommending not bilingualism but equal validity for Welsh with English in Wales. The result of this report was the Welsh Language Act of 1967. Equal validity, as explained in the report, required "a clear, positive, legislative declaration of general application to the effect that any act, writing or thing done in Welsh in Wales ... should have the like legal force as if it had been done in English" (quoted in R. Lewis, 1969, pp. 27–28). Although the general principle was strong, the Act only implemented it in very precisely delineated areas and, furthermore, no mechanism to compel government agencies to adhere to it was provided (R. Lewis, 1969, pp. 35–38).

Even so, the 1967 Act proved a valuable resource for the language movement. For example, the principle of equal validity was cited by the

1972 Bowen Committee Report as its primary reason for recommending bilingual road signs, with Welsh given priority, throughout Wales (Great Britain, 1972, p. 64). This report was virtually a complete victory for Cymdeithas yr Iaith, and although the road-signs campaign was renewed, due to delays in implementing its recommendations, the changeover to bilingual signs soon progressed to the point that anyone traveling even a short distance anywhere in Wales would see some evidence of the official status of the Welsh language there. Cymdeithas yr Iaith campaigns affected other areas of public life as well: they applied pressure for the provision of government forms in Welsh, for extended use of Welsh in law courts, and for recognition of the right of individuals to correspond with government agencies in Welsh. In fact, in virtually all areas of contact with the central state or local government, the official status of the Welsh language was asserted, and the gains made over the first two decades of the Society's existence, both in the language's visibility and its recognition by officialdom, were substantial.

Although initially the relationship between Cymdeithas yr Iaith and Plaid Cymru was close, the increasing use of illegal, though nonviolent, forms of protest by Cymdeithas yr Iaith brought accusations from Plaid Cymru leaders that its activities were harming their electoral prospects. Plaid Cymru's members, on the whole, were unwilling to participate in such activity, which entailed considerable vocational and social risks for them; for Cymdeithas members, mainly university students who had greater control over how they used their time and who were not yet launched on a career, the risks were less.

In spite of these accusations, Plaid Cymru clearly benefitted from the outcome of Cymdeithas campaigns, which succeeded in winning government recognition, publicly displayed, for the primary carrier of a distinct Welsh identity. Furthermore, the clarification, even polarization, of attitudes about the Welsh language that was forced upon all political parties in Wales as a consequence of public reaction to Cymdeithas campaigns made it far more difficult for them to appeal to their Welsh identity without being willing to support concrete measures to aid the language. [See Green (1982) on the political appeal of ethnic identity; also cf. Iwan (1981) pp. 49–50.] Finally, the actual act of campaigning for specific attainable measures to reverse the decline of the Welsh language improved morale within the broader nationalist movement and served to objectify the more general struggle for Welsh self-government. In the words of one Cymdeithas member, the language campaign managed "to inject a new reality into nationalism by bringing to light through the language struggle the hidden oppression in the relationship of Wales with England" (C. Davies, 1973, p. 249).

A few Plaid Cymru leaders eventually acknowledged that Cymdeithas yr Iaith had contributed significantly to the party during this period. Emrys Roberts, one of the Blaid's national officers in 1977, stated,

It was the activities of Cymdeithas yr Iaith and even the more extreme groups that revived interest in nationalism and made Welshness an issue again. The revival in 1966 can be traced directly to these activities. [Interview, 26 March 1977]

The more extreme groups referred to, also active in the 1960s, adopted violent forms of protest, setting bombs in public buildings and on water pipelines, methods from which both Cymdeithas yr Iaith and Plaid Cymru dissociated themselves. The group that received the most media attention was an organization calling itself the Free Wales Army, which reportedly held military maneuvers and claimed to have a supply of weapons. The actual membership of these groups was extremely small. The activities of the most effective of them, Mudiad Amddiffyn Cymru (The Movement for the Defense of Wales), were stopped by the arrest and conviction of a single individual.[8] Probably the major factor in ending these violent protests by the early 1970s was the success of Cymdeithas yr Iaith campaigns and the electoral victories of Plaid Cymru.

The period following the 1979 defeat of the Labour government's proposed Assembly for Wales bore some resemblance to that of the early 1960s. After a little over a decade of electoral successes, the likelihood of achieving nationalist aims through conventional political means again appeared remote. The general dismay in nationalist ranks was deepened by the 1979 general election results, when Plaid Cymru's share of the poll fell in most constituencies and its president, Gwynfor Evans, lost his parliamentary seat. In these circumstances, a number of groups using violence against property, with an element of danger to the general public, reappeared. The particular issue which stimulated their activities was a language-related problem, namely, the increasing numbers of second and retirement homes, mostly owned by English city dwellers, in Welsh-speaking areas. The percentage of such homes, which were unoccupied for most of the year, was so high as to virtually destroy the social life of many Welsh-speaking communities.[9] Cymdeithas yr Iaith had campaigned on this issue for many years, by occupying second homes and disrupting auctions of such properties. However, in the spring of 1980, a series of deliberately set, holiday-home fires began to occur. No single organization appeared to be responsible and the perpetrators remained remarkably elusive.

In spite of the similarities with the early 1960s, Plaid Cymru's response to these more direct forms of nationalist activism in the post-Referendum period demonstrated a greater degree of confidence than previously.

Although condemning the use of violence, Plaid Cymru leaders appeared relatively unconcerned that the activities of these extremist groups would damage the party politically. On the contrary, they accused the government of stimulating such actions by its insensitivity to Welsh problems. Commenting after the Welsh Office had turned down all proposals made by Plaid-dominated Gwynedd County Council on ways to curb the spread of second homes there, Dafydd Elis Thomas (Plaid Cymru MP for Merioneth) said, "It is dangerous to go on ignoring a problem to the point that violence becomes an established element in the situation" (quoted in *The Observer*, 11 April 1982; also see *Western Mail*, 9 February 1982).

A further indication of the Blaid's recognition of the contribution of language activism to the movement was a new willingness not only to sanction, but to undertake nonviolent direct action. Within a year of the 1979 set-backs, the party was involved in an effective and eventually successful campaign of civil disobedience on behalf of the Welsh language. The specific issue was the effort to ensure that a new fourth television channel, being introduced throughout Britain, be made available for a full Welsh-language television service in Wales. This particular issue was one on which Cymdeithas yr Iaith had campaigned for years using techniques such as climbing television masts to prevent broadcasting and destroying broadcasting equipment. Various government reports, investigating the potential uses of the fourth channel, had come out in favor of the proposal for a Welsh-language television station,[10] and, by the spring of 1979, all major political parties were committed to its implementation. However, in September 1979 the newly elected Conservative government reversed its position on the fourth channel in Wales, declaring that while the number of hours of Welsh programming broadcast each week would be increased, these would continue to be distributed across several channels and there would be no official Welsh-language service. Plaid Cymru asserted that this decision illustrated yet again that Wales would never receive fair treatment from any London government, even on an issue such as this where Welsh opinion was largely united. The Blaid claimed to represent the views of both Welsh and English speakers, maintaining that most English speakers favored moving all Welsh programs to the fourth channel in order to avoid interruptions in English-language programming on the other channels.

Then, in the spring of 1980, Plaid Cymru president Gwynfor Evans announced his intention to fast, to the death if necessary, unless the government honored its original pledge on the fourth channel. He proposed to begin his fast in October. Over the summer, a series of public meetings and demonstrations revealed massive support for his position. In addition, Plaid Cymru orchestrated a campaign of civil disobedience in which nearly two thousand people refused to pay their television license fees. When, in September, the government made an about-face and acquiesced in the demand for a Welsh channel, the secretary of state for Wales acknowledged that "the fundamental reason for the change is that we failed to persuade moderate, middle-ground opinoion [sic], most of the media, and the centre ground in Wales that our judgement was right" (quoted in *Western Mail*, 18 September 1980).

This extraordinary victory over a strongly entrenched government greatly revived spirits among party members and fuelled a growing inclination to place more emphasis on direct action in nationalist campaigns. This shift in tactics was formalized in the 1981 report of the Special Commission set up by the party to recommend future directions in the wake of the 1979 setbacks. The report argued that "while Plaid Cymru should continue to conceive of itself as the political arm of the nationalist movement, it must also be prepared to give the lead to the movement as a whole" (Plaid Cymru, 1981b, p. 24). Giving such a lead was expected to involve the party in pressure-group tactics, such as "the organisation of petitions, demonstrations, marches, sit-ins" and possibly in illegal activities; "we should not regard laws imposed on us from outside as sacrosanct if it is necessary to infringe them in order to safeguard the interests of Wales or Welsh communities" (Plaid Cymru, 1981b, p. 26). However, Plaid Cymru's success in transforming itself into a mainstream political party restricted its ability to produce activists for campaigns of civil disobedience; subsequently, the party limited itself to one other major campaign involving illegal acts, namely, that to secure equalization of water rates between England and Wales.

The Welsh language has thus been of central importance to the contemporary nationalist movement in Wales. While some have depicted it as a problem for the movement, it is apparent, on balance, that it has been of immense benefit to Welsh political nationalism. Its victories provided almost the first official governmental reinforcement of Welsh identity since the sixteenth century. The dynamic of campaigning on specific language issues created a wider awareness that there were areas of Welsh life in which the British state actively opposed manifestations of a separate Welsh identity; and it gave a vital boost to nationalist morale during at least two periods when electoral politics seemed to be leading nowhere. Although other organizations, primarily Cymdeithas yr Iaith, actually developed these positive aspects of the language issue, by the end of the 1970s Plaid Cymru felt secure enough in conventional electoral politics in Wales that it assumed a more active role in the final stages of one major language campaign. The Blaid's 1981 Special Commission recognized the potential contributions of the language struggle when it suggested that, in a broader European context, minority languages "will become an important weapon in the battle between centralism and decentralism" (Plaid Cymru, 1981b,

p. 9). And even the Commission's minority report, prepared by former party chairman Phil Williams, which warned of the potential divisiveness of the language, nevertheless also contended that it is the party's "major source of strength" and that "the greatest challenge Plaid Cymru faces in the next ten years is to find a way to use the strength of the Welsh language to serve the whole of Wales" (Plaid Cymru, 1981b, p. 100).

THE GROWTH OF A LANGUAGE-BASED INFRASTRUCTURE

One way in which the Welsh language had already been enlisted to serve the whole of Wales was in the creation of a Welsh infrastructure within the British state. The nature of Wales's incorporation by England was such that, by the nineteenth century, no formal institutional distinctions remained between them. The most salient difference was the existence of separate languages. The Welsh language subsequently provided the primary basis for the growth of a Welsh infrastructure within, and related to, the British bureaucracy.

Education is one of the principal areas in which linguistic differences may stimulate organizational distinctions. Since education was also one of the first areas of social welfare into which the modern state extended its influence, minority groups with distinct viable languages have possessed an important resource in their struggle for special recognition within the expanding bureaucracy. However, the way in which this resource was used determined whether the group's separate linguistic identity was protected or weakened. In the last century, the Welsh elite used the Welsh language to obtain an educational system in Wales considered superior to that in England. However, these educational advances proved ultimately harmful to the cause of Welsh-language maintenance. Although the government was persuaded to cease active opposition to the use of the Welsh language in schools, the Welsh elite argued their case on the grounds that the language had to be used to initiate monolingual Welsh-speaking children into an educational system that was English both in language and in its cultural orientation (Jenkins & Ramage, 1951, pp. 210–215). Thus, the progress made in the first quarter of the twentieth century in introducing Welsh into the elementary schools was misleading insofar as its contribution to the maintenance of the Welsh language was concerned. While Welsh was used in most primary schools in Welsh-speaking areas as the main medium of instruction and was taught as a subject in many secondary schools, the perceived purpose of education was the development of facility in the English language (J. L. Williams, 1973).

The first school that used Welsh as its principal medium of instruction in order to safeguard the language and foster Welsh culture was a private venture begun in 1939. The immediate impetus for establishing the

Aberystwyth Welsh School was the influx of wartime evacuees from Liverpool, whose presence in the area tended to reduce the use of Welsh in the public schools. The school's founder, Ifan ab Owen Edwards, who also founded Urdd Gobaith Cymru, a Welsh youth organization, wanted to ensure that his son would receive his education in Welsh and with emphasis on Welsh culture (G. Davies, 1973, pp. 75–77). The Aberystwyth Welsh School was an academic success, but its financial position, as a private venture, was always insecure. The school's primary contribution to the postwar development of the Welsh schools movement was to demonstrate the feasibility of Welsh-medium education and, through the support given it by middle-class parents, to help dispel fears that children in such a school might be retarded in general academic growth. However, the pattern of private education could not be widely emulated in Wales as a practical means of improving the position of the Welsh language in the schools.

The government inadvertently provided a new resource, in the form of the 1944 Education Act, to those eager to establish Welsh-medium education. Although the Act did not deal with the language of instruction, it directed that authorities endeavor, insofar as practicable, to educate children in accordance with the wishes of their parents. Under this provision, Welsh parents were able to force local education authorities to begin setting up Welsh-medium primary schools in non–Welsh-speaking areas or areas in which Welsh was under pressure. By 1948, the first such schools had been established at Cardiff, Llanelli, and Llandudno by groups encouraged by Ifan ab Owen Edwards and by Norah Isaac, the headmistress of the Aberystwyth Welsh School. At the same time, in a move not directly stimulated by them, the local authority in Flintshire established Welsh-medium schools at Rhyl, Mold, and Holywell (G. Davies, 1973, p. 154; J. L. Williams, 1973, p. 101).

The Welsh schools movement was so successful that by 1965 there were 34 Welsh-medium primary schools with about 4,000 pupils; by 1974, the numbers of pupils had doubled, and growth continued unabated.[11] The rapid growth of the primary schools led to the establishment of Welsh-medium secondary schools and to demands, which remained unmet, for a Welsh-medium university college.[12] Initially, Welsh-medium schools were intended to serve Welsh-speaking children who lived in non–Welsh-speaking areas. However, the leadership given from the Welsh-speaking professional middle class—and the high academic standing established by the new schools—soon widened the appeal of Welsh-medium education, and these schools began accepting children from English-speaking homes (Great Britain, 1967, p. 222). This trend continued so that by 1980 one such school, newly opened in the Rhondda, a working-class area in the southeast, had not a single child from a

Welsh-speaking home; and one of the first of the Welsh-medium secondary schools, Ysgol Gyfun Rhydfelen (established in 1962), had over 90 percent of its intake from non–Welsh-speaking homes.

A major factor in the movement's success in bringing children of non–Welsh-speaking parents into the Welsh schools was the work of Mudiad Ysgolion Meithrin (The Welsh Nursery Schools Movement). This organization, established in 1971, was a private charity, but it received grants, in steadily increasing amounts, from the Welsh Office.[13] The organizers of Mudiad Ysgolion Meithrin were conscious of their evangelizing role in the movement, and they put pressure on education authorities to ensure that the numbers of Welsh-medium primary schools would be adequate to meet the demand being created by the Welsh playgroups. Furthermore, since the cooperation of parents was required to establish a playgroup, each new group tended to create a core of activists for the Welsh schools movement. In the words of one of the officers of Mudiad Ysgolion Meithrin, "The parents work together to raise money for the playgroup, and it is natural that they would work together to get more Welsh-medium primary schools when their children are ready for that" (interview, 4 May 1977).

Of particular significance in the growth of the Welsh schools movement was the fact that it was based largely in the non–Welsh-speaking areas, and only after its establishment there did it begin to affect education in predominantly Welsh-speaking parts of Wales, where English still predominated in the schools. The experience of the Welsh-medium schools in dealing with children from English-speaking homes had increasing relevance for education authorities in Welsh-speaking areas who were struggling, from the 1970s, to absorb large numbers of English immigrants without consequent loss of the Welsh language in the local schools. In addition, the demand for Welsh-medium secondary education spread into the Welsh-speaking areas once the viability of teaching virtually all subjects through the medium of Welsh had been demonstrated by the Welsh-medium secondary schools in non–Welsh-speaking parts of Wales. Thus the Welsh schools movement became a source of unity and common purpose for groups throughout Wales.

The Welsh language was also a major factor in the growth of a Welsh-based educational infrastructure, another development that helped unify Welsh- and non–Welsh-speaking areas. One of the most important of the Welsh educational organizations within the bureaucracy was the Welsh Joint Education Committee, established in 1948 under the 1944 Education Act (Khleif, 1975, pp. 184–187). This body was responsible for preparing course syllabi and setting examinations for schools in Wales. The need for a separate examination board for Wales was reinforced by the growing demand for materials and examinations in Welsh in most subjects as a consequence of the success of the Welsh schools movement. This demand was also the main reason for the establishment in 1964 of a permanent Committee for Wales within the British Schools Council, an organization to develop and evaluate educational materials and programs. The Committee for Wales was the only subcommittee of the Council based on a geographic area, rather than a subject area or age group (J. L. Williams, 1976). Each devolution of authority tended to stimulate others, and the 1970 placement of the Welsh Department of Education under the Welsh Office represented a major development in the Welsh educational infrastructure.

Outside the bureaucracy but directly stimulated by it was the growth of Undeb Cenedlaethol Athrawon Cymru (The National Association of the Teachers of Wales, or UCAC). UCAC was established in 1940 by a few individuals who supported an independent system of education for Wales. The association identified itself with the language movement, making the furtherance of the Welsh language and culture a part of its official constitution (D. G. Jones, 1973b, pp. 293–294; Undeb Cenedlaethol Athrawon Cymru, 1977, p. 2). UCAC remained a very small organization and was ignored by the official establishment until the late 1960s. However, its membership began to grow with successful recruitment among the staff of the Welsh-medium schools as well as in schools in the political nationalist stronghold of northwest Wales. By the 1970s, it was able to secure representation on various government bodies concerned with education, namely, the Welsh Joint Education Committee and the education committees of the local authorities, and it began to act more like a trade union.

With the growth of the welfare bureaucracy after World War II, many organizations were created, within the bureaucracy or in areas related to it, which found their rationale, in whole or in part, in the Welsh language (Table 3.2 enumerates a few of them). Such organizations were of great significance to the nationalist movement, both in heightening the sense of Welsh identity and in bringing decision-making powers to Welsh bodies.

Nationalism's opponents were not unaware of the implications for separatism lodged in the creation of a Welsh infrastructure, and they often resisted this process. There was, for example, considerable opposition within the Labour Party to the Labour government's decision to place the Welsh Department of Education under the Welsh Office (Rowlands, 1972, p. 335). Many of the difficulties nationalists faced following the 1979 general election stemmed from the Conservative government's efforts to dismantle much of the British welfare bureaucracy. Within the educational infrastructure itself, for example, the government's elimination of the Schools Council simultaneously eliminated that organization's Welsh

Table 3.2
Organizations in the Welsh-language Infrastructure

Name of Organization	Description
Yr Academi Gymreig	The Welsh Academy. Founded 1959 for the purpose of literary patronage. Received Welsh Arts Council support.
BBC Radio Cymru	Established 1935. Welsh service expanded 1977.
BBC Teledu Cymru	Established 1964. Provided Welsh-language programs for television.
Bwrdd Ffilmiau Cymraeg	The Welsh Films Board. Established 1972 to produce Welsh-language films. Received Welsh Arts Council support.
Cwmni Theatr Cymru	Theater Company of Wales. Established 1967 to produce Welsh-language drama. Received Welsh Arts Council support.
S4C	Sianel Pedwar Cymru, the Welsh fourth television channel. Began broadcasting in November 1982. Enabled the growth of numerous independent Welsh television production companies.
Welsh Arts Council	Formed 1967 from the Welsh Committee of the Arts Council of Great Britain. Its Literature Committee supported Welsh-language writers and publishers.
Welsh Books Council	Established 1963. Received Welsh Arts Council support beginning 1970. Assisted in production, marketing, and distribution of Welsh books.

(Continued)

Table 3.2
(Continued)

Name of Organization	Description
Welsh Language Council	Advisory panel, established by the Welsh Office in 1973, abolished 1978.
Welsh Language Education Development Committee	Established 1986 under the Welsh Joint Education Committee to coordinate developments in Welsh-medium education.
Welsh National Language Unit	Established 1968 by the Welsh Joint Education Committee to develop programs for teaching Welsh.

Committee, a body that had been gradually acquiring a degree of autonomy. Political nationalists were critical of the trend to reduce the powers of Welsh-based organizations, even when they did not consider the organizations themselves to be particularly supportive of Welsh interests. Of greater importance in resisting the dismantling of the Welsh infrastructure was the opposition of vested interests within the establishment unwilling to see their own power base weakened.

SUMMARY

The Welsh experience strongly suggests that the possession of a separate language represents a source of great potential strength for an ethnic group. A distinctive national language, far from being merely a mark of group identity, may make a substantive contribution to nationalist political movements. Whether or not it does so depends as much on the attitudes of the ethnic elite and on other external resources as it does on the numerical strength of the language. In nineteenth-century Wales, while numbers of Welsh speakers increased, the Welsh elite treated the language as a handicap. In the twentieth century, while the language came under an increasingly obvious threat to its very survival, it emerged as an effective basis for nationalist mobilization. Its preservation provided a central tenet in the nationalist case for self-government. The struggle for linguistic rights helped objectify the nationalist argument about 'English oppression,' and the considerable successes of the language movement brought official recognition for Welsh identity. Finally, in spite of its status, since the

1920s, as a minority language even within Wales, it provided a basis for the development of a Welsh educational system and the achievement of a degree of administrative unity for Wales within the British state.

NOTES

1. During its first two decades, the party was called Plaid Genedlaethol Cymru or the Welsh Nationalist Party. In the mid-1940s, its name became simply Plaid Cymru. This is translated as the party of Wales, but no English version of the name is used.

2. The six founders of the Welsh Nationalist Party were: Moses Gruffydd, a university agricultural scientist; Fred Jones, a Congregationalist minister; H. R. Jones, a sales representative; Saunders Lewis, a university lecturer; Lewis Valentine, a Baptist minister; and D. E. Williams, a carpenter.

3. In the 1940s, concern for the economic well-being of Wales was added to the second goal, while the third objective became membership in the United Nations. See Chapter Four for a discussion of the changes in the aims made by the 1981 and 1982 Annual Conferences.

4. Plaid Cymru owed part of its high vote to the fact that two of the four by-elections (one in north Wales, three in the southeast) in 1945 and 1946 were straight fights: in the north Wales constituency of Caernarfon Boroughs in 1945, only the Liberal Party and Plaid Cymru contested the seat, and in Ogmore in 1946, only the Labour Party and Plaid Cymru put up candidates. Furthermore, in the by-election in Neath in 1945, the only party contesting the seat besides Plaid Cymru and the Labour Party was the Revolutionary Communist Party, which came third in the poll. However, Plaid Cymru was second, ahead of the Conservative Party, in Aberdare in 1946, a performance that compared favorably with its third-place finish behind both Labour and Conservative candidates in the two by-elections in southeast valley constituencies that were held in the following two decades (in Pontypool in 1958 and in Abertillery in 1965).

5. Leo Abse, Labour MP for Pontypool, exploited such fears during the 1979 referendum campaign for an Assembly for Wales by raising the spectre of an Assembly dominated by Welsh speakers from the north and west riding roughshod over the interests of the English-speaking majority in the southeast. Abse began attacking the proposed Assembly on linguistic grounds even before a referendum was mooted.

> Mr. Abse predicted the 'Welsh-speaking bureaucratic elite' would become a 'praetorian guard.' Assembly men would exercise their undoubted right to speak in Welsh both inside the Assembly and to officials.
> 'Of course, why not?' he said. 'If you create a Welsh Assembly that is a right they must have ... but if you exercise it you must have officials who understand what they say.
> 'They will so exercise it that it will be a precondition for entry into the Welsh Civil Service that you will have to be Welsh. Men and women from Gwent, Cardiff, and Glamorgan will find that they have no role to play' (*Western Mail*, 16 November 1977).

6. This demonstration followed another sit-down demonstration in the town's post office earlier in the day which had also failed to produce any arrests.

7. Geraint Jones, the Society's secretary at the time.

8. John Jenkins, who was sentenced to a ten-year prison term in 1969.

9. A 1982 survey (*The Observer*, 14 February 1982) revealed that there were 8,000 second homes in Dyfed in west Wales; thus there were more such homes in this single county in Wales than there were in all of Scotland. In many villages in Gwynedd, in northwest Wales, second homes constituted up to one-half of the total housing stock, and there was at least one example of a village made up entirely of second homes.

10. The Crawford Report in 1973 and the Annan Report in 1977.

11. In Mid Glamorgan, a predominantly non–Welsh-speaking county in southeast Wales, the number of pupils in Welsh-medium primary schools in 1974 represented 3.8 percent of the total school population (Betts, 1976, p. 78).

12. The first Welsh-medium secondary school (Ysgol Glan Clwyd) was established in Flint in 1956 with 93 pupils and had grown to 850 pupils by 1973 (Cymdeithas yr Iaith Gymraeg, 1974).

13. Its first grant came in 1973 in the amount of £5,500. The amount had risen to £217,000 for 1981 (Mudiad Ysgolion Meithrin Cymraeg, 1975–76, p. 10; *Western Mail*, 16 April 1980).

4

Toward a Welsh Economy

Although minority nationalities base their identity on their distinctive cultures and unique historical experiences, there is a degree to which the maintenance of these identities is facilitated by external economic forces. In such circumstances, some elements of the national identity are imposed on the ethnic population rather than being in any sense generated from within it. The nature and degree of influence these external economic forces exert on national identity depends largely on the manner and timing of the incorporation of the ethnic region by the state.

Many of the historic national communities in western European states were absorbed by an expanding core region quite early in the process of state formation. During the Middle Ages, they served the state as food producers, as sources of revenue and military recruits, and as areas for colonization usually via large land grants to a feudal elite. This pattern of a politically and socially dominant core drawing sustenance from relatively powerless peripheral regions was reinforced by the development of industrial capitalism. Few peripheral regions had a native elite economically prosperous enough to establish a regional capitalist base. Thus these regions quickly fell under the economic control of those who could draw on the accumulated wealth of the core. The economic arrangements thereby imposed on the periphery were particularly severe if the region contained mineral resources needed to fuel the new industries. In these cases, extractive industry was developed in the periphery, and the wealth generated there was funnelled to financial centers in the core. The cultural distinctiveness of the periphery was commonly used to explain the lack of native economic development and to justify its exploitation by the state elite.

This pattern was repeated in many essential respects as the capitalist states began to acquire world empires. The human and material resources of colonies in the Third World were used to enrich both individual capitalists and the imperialist states. And the alleged 'cultural backwardness' of the colonies was proffered to explain their relative poverty and their inability to develop their own resources, as well as to justify colonial conquest as a means of bringing them the benefits of Western civilization. The overseas colonies generally experienced greater oppression, particularly at the level of overt legal discrimination, than had peripheral regions within the boundaries of the colonial states. However, the similarity of their experiences gave birth to the argument that these peripheral regions were the first colonies, and remained internal colonies, of the imperial capitalist states.

Since viable ethnic nationalist movements exist in areas that were not internal colonies, internal colonialism cannot be taken as a straightforwad explanation of ethnic nationalism (cf. Clark, 1980; Douglass & da Silva, 1971; Pi-Sunyer, 1980). However, the consequences of the special type of economic exploitation endured by internal colonies deeply affected the character of nationalist movements that subsequently arose in some of these areas. The economic history of Wales provides a classic example of an internal colony, and the effects of internal colonialism on the Welsh nationalist movement were profound. Welsh nationalist leaders responded first to the cultural denigration that was an integral part of the internal colonial experience. With the growth of the welfare state in the post–World War II era, the state elite attempted to alleviate the worst effects of this form of economic repression, and, in so doing, they inadvertently strengthened the political nationalist position when they introduced programs for regional economic planning. In fact, the provisions made for regional planning were closely linked to the growth in popular support for the nationalist movement in the late 1960s. A third effect of Wales's internal colonial experience on the nationalist movement was to propel it gradually toward an increasingly socialist position as nationalists came to comprehend more fully the economic, social, and cultural legacy of internal colonialism.

ECONOMIC HISTORY OF AN INTERNAL COLONY

The concept of internal colonialism was developed by analogy to the overseas colonialism of imperialist states. Thus it was not defined in terms of a few essential features but rather was broadly described by the complex of interrelated factors, both economic and social, that facilitated the systematic siphoning of wealth from a periphery to the core (cf. Hechter, 1975, p. 33). Nevertheless, two criteria were universally present in regions that were considered to be internal colonies. First, an instrumental relationship existed between the core region and its internal colonies in that decisions were made, by the state's ruling elite, to serve the interests of the core without regard for detrimental effects on the peripheral economy and society (cf. Balandier, 1966). Second, the peripheral region had a separate culture from the core, and cultural distinctions provided a basis for socioeconomic divisions, with the economic dependency of the periphery being largely attributed to its cultural distinctiveness. This association of economic deprivation with cultural differences produced a sense of inferiority among the ethnic population and often induced them to attempt to eradicate the cultural traits on which they blamed their economic difficulties. Ethnic leaders frequently responded in this manner, especially if they could thereby pass into the ranks of the state elite. Ethnic nationalist leaders, in contrast, while also perceiving the links between their nation's economic and cultural status, sought to reverse the process by revaluing the culture and using it as a basis for political mobilization to redress the economic balance.

In the century and a half prior to World War II, the Welsh economy was a typical example of internal colonialism. The Industrial Revolution began in south Wales in the mid-eighteenth century with the opening, in Merthyr Tydfil, of the first of its major iron-smelting operations. The iron industry expanded along the northern rim of the coalfield to take advantage of available coal and limestone as well as iron ore. Iron output increased fivefold between 1820 and 1860, and, for most of those years, south Wales's iron output was the largest of any region in Britain (Driscoll, 1962, p. 114). While Welsh mineral resources and manpower were essential ingredients in Britain's early industrialization, the Welsh iron industry itself was in the hands of English entrepreneurs who had developed it using external sources of finance (Minchinton, 1969, p. xvii). Welsh iron ore was unsuitable for new steel-making processes introduced in the 1850s, and the industry began to depend on foreign ore. The location of the iron industries at the heads of the valleys thus became disadvantageous, and many plants moved closer to the ports (Minchinton, 1964, pp. 12–14). However, the south Wales valleys were saved temporarily from the consequences of their dependence on a single industry by the growing economic importance of coal, which assumed the central position in the economy of south Wales during the second half of the nineteenth century (Minchinton, 1964, p. 10).

The coal industry, in contrast to the iron industry, was developed largely by Welsh entrepreneurs. However, this industry soon fell under the control of a few large companies, with the result that it drew capital out of Wales, and the Welsh industrial base did not diversify[1] (England, 1972, pp. 31–32). Furthermore, the coal industry came to be largely dependent on the export market. In 1860, 1.7 million tons (17 percent of total production) were mined for export; by 1913, the peak year, 37 million tons (65 percent) were exported. The drastic contraction of the export market beginning in the 1920s started the decline of the industry. By 1945, export coal had fallen to its 1860 level of 1.7 million tons, and this amount represented only 8 percent of total production (L. Jones, 1962, pp. 87, 91).

Rural Wales served the Welsh iron and coal industries as a source of labor.[2] In the half century from 1861 to 1911, the demand for labor in these industries was so high that not only did the south Wales valleys absorb most of the surplus Welsh rural population of nearly 400,000 people, they also attracted large numbers of English and Irish workers (B. Thomas, 1962, 1969).

Thus, the characteristic economic pattern of an internal colony was established in Wales. The south Wales economy was heavily dependent on a single extractive industry tied to the export market; profits from the use of this resource were channelled out of Wales by an industrial structure centered on London. Most of the rest of Wales, which could have benefitted from capital investment, quickly became an industrial backwater, serving only as a supply of abundant labor.[3] Overall Welsh economic development was stunted in comparison to England (cf. Friedlander, 1970); there was little indigenous industry, and the infrastructure was oriented to extraction of mineral resources rather than distribution within the region.

Welsh over-dependence on the export market was, in large measure, a consequence of the British government's long adherence to the economic doctrine of laissez faire and its derivative policy of free trade. This policy, which was not finally abandoned until 1931, was particularly advantageous to the British state given its early industrialization and control of maritime commerce. It was also advantageous to the London financial institutions, whose dominance over world finance was as important to the British economy as was British industry (Hobsbawm, 1968, pp. 206–207). However, over-development of the export sector created, in the Welsh economy, serious vulnerability to fluctuations in the world market. Loss of coal markets in Canada and Europe shortly after World War I was devastating to south Wales. Unemployment became chronic, reaching 16 percent in 1927 and 38 percent in 1932 at the depth of the depression. Some areas, such as Merthyr Tydfil and the Rhondda, had unemployment rates of over 50 percent of the insured male working population (G. L. Rees, 1972, pp. 62–63; B. Thomas, 1962, pp. 55–56). One response was massive emigration: Wales lost a total of 450,000 people between 1921 and 1939, most of them going to England (B. Thomas, 1962, pp. 13, 18). The economic system that internal colonialism had created in Wales left it incapable of any effective internal response to the crisis (Humphrys, 1972, p. 32).

The British government did not abandon its policy of nonintervention in the economy until forced to do so by the necessities of total war. The first substantial improvement in employment in Wales came with the outbreak of World War II, when the government transferred many strategic industries to safer locations in the western part of Britain. As a result, south Wales gained a number of new factories that were to provide a base for postwar expansion. The government's commitment to welfare programs by the end of the war meant that its role in the economy had to expand as it sought to prevent a recurrence of the economic disaster that had followed World War I. The end result, in Wales, was to be an attenuation of many of the social and economic indicators of an internal colony. However, Welsh economic dependence on the core would not be fundamentally altered.

In 1945, the government passed the Distribution of Industries Act, which provided positive incentives for firms to locate in Wales and also restrained the further development of manufacturing industry in London and the Midlands. As a result, by 1947, 500 new factories had been established under the auspices of the Welsh office of the Board of Trade. The rate of approval slowed somewhat in the next two years, but, even so, by the early 1950s enough new industry had been attracted to Wales to have reduced unemployment to a very low level (2.8 percent in December 1951). Since the government perceived the primary purpose of the special programs for Development Areas to be the reduction of unemployment, rather than the establishment of a balanced regional economy, it responded to the improved employment figures by dropping restrictions on industry locating in southern England. As a consequence, the siting of new factories in Wales virtually ceased in the 1950s (Manners, 1964, pp. 45–47).

Rising levels of unemployment during the late 1950s once again stimulated government activity on behalf of peripheral areas. The Local Employment Act of 1960 reinforced the basic scheme of incentives for new industries, but it was applied to newly designated Development Districts instead of the older and much larger Development Areas. Uncertainty as to which locations qualified as Development Districts nullified whatever positive benefits might have accrued from the Act (Davies & Thomas, 1976, p. 28). Broader Development Areas were reinstituted in 1966 by the Industrial Investment Act, and the Regional Employment Premium, which was in effect a direct labor subsidy, was introduced in 1967. These two events marked the start of the second postwar period of industrial expansion in Wales.

While successive postwar governments concentrated on the reduction of unemployment in industrial areas, programs for rural areas were aimed primarily at stimulating production. Welsh rural areas were first affected by government economic programs in 1933, when the government launched its Milk Marketing Scheme, which introduced collection of milk at a guaranteed price from farms previously dependent on the sale of butter. The scheme made conversion to the sale of liquid milk almost the only profitable choice for Welsh dairy farmers and, in the process, profoundly altered Welsh farm life (Ashby & Evans, 1944, p. 108; David Jenkins, 1971, pp. 252, 261–264). The concept of guaranteed prices was extended to most other farm products by the Agriculture Act of 1947. The resultant production grants represented over one-third of net farm income in Wales in the early 1970s, as compared to less than one-fourth in Great Britain as a whole (Matthews, 1971, p. 13).

There was virtually no integration of rural and industrial economic development programs. The government's first attempt to develop an integrated economic plan for Wales was the 1967 White Paper, *Wales: The Way Ahead*, prepared by the Welsh Office for inclusion in an overall British plan. The document was widely criticized as inadequate for detailed economic planning and overly optimistic in its projection of the number of jobs that would be available in Wales (Osmond, 1974, pp. 108–109). Aside from asserting that *Wales: The Way Ahead* should provide the basis for the development of individual economic plans by the county councils, the government did little else to encourage comprehensive economic planning for Wales until 1976, when it established the Welsh Development Agency (WDA). Although the WDA had a broad mandate to direct economic development in Wales (Great Britain, 1975b, p. 1), in practice its responsibilities were limited to coordination and implementation of existing government policy for regional industrial development and its planning capability was correspondingly restricted (Osmond, 1977, pp. 213–217).

Thus, in the decades after World War II, government programs brought new industry to Wales, reduced unemployment, and helped to diversify the economic base, thereby ameliorating many of the consequences of its internal colonial past. The relationship between core and periphery no longer appeared purely instrumental. Nor was there an obvious cultural division of labor. Nevertheless, there were signs that the basic economic dependency and vulnerability of an internal colony had not been fundamentally altered in Wales by central government programs. Although the Welsh economy was more diversified (Conkling, 1964; G. L. Rees, 1972, pp. 64–65), by 1973 Wales still had 19.2 percent of its male work force employed in only two industrial categories, namely, mining/ quarrying and metal manufacture, as compared to 5.8 percent for the

United Kingdom (Great Britain, 1975a, p. 68). Thus, for men at least, the Welsh economy remained relatively specialized. Many of the new industries attracted to Wales employed primarily women (K. O. Morgan, 1982, pp. 351–352; G. A. Williams, 1982) and could not absorb the large numbers of coal and steel workers whose jobs were being eliminated. As a result, even during the period of greatest prosperity in the postwar years, Wales continued to have relatively high unemployment and low economic activity rates compared to Britain as a whole (Manners, 1964, pp. 32–34).

Postwar industrial growth in Wales was largely financed and controlled by outside capital. A large proportion of the new factories established in Wales were owned by foreign firms (G. Davies & Thomas, 1976) and many of the remainder had their origins in southeastern England. By 1973, 75 percent of Welsh firms with 100 or more employees had their head offices outside Wales (Tomkins & Lovering, 1973). As a consequence, when economic recession took hold in the late 1970s, Wales experienced a far higher rate of factory closures and job losses than did southern England, due to the large number of branch factories that constituted the Welsh industrial base.

Thus, the basic dependency of the Welsh economy was not eliminated during the postwar period, in spite of the great improvement in employment levels and standard of living that was effected by the new programs of the welfare state. Government regional development programs offered economic incentives for industries to locate some of their productive activities in peripheral regions. Typically, the activities transferred to Wales required semi-skilled or unskilled labor; administration, research, and development usually remained in the prosperous core area. The state elite did not encourage the development of an integrated regional economic base that might be able to reduce Welsh economic dependency. Their reluctance in this regard was manifested in their uncoordinated approach to economic programs for Welsh rural and industrial areas, in the tardiness and the inadequacy of the economic planning documents produced, and in their unwillingness to empower regionally based bodies to plan for integrated economic development.

NATIONALIST RESPONSE

Ethnic nationalist movements in internal colonies were not straightforward responses to the circumstances of their economic dependency. The internal colonial pattern in Wales was apparent in the nineteenth century, but the nationalist movement of that period ignored both the nature and consequences of Welsh industrialization. The Welsh Nationalist Party, which as Plaid Cymru was to become the central organization in twentieth-century Welsh nationalism, was established just as the worst effects of economic dependency were being realized in Wales. Yet its founders had not been primarily motivated by such economic problems, and the party itself attracted very little popular support in its early years. Instead of stimulating a popular movement toward nationalist politics, the experience of the depression brought the consolidation of British-based class politics in south Wales. Plaid Cymru's greatest internal growth and popular appeal came in two postwar periods—the mid-1940s and the decade from 1966 to 1976—when government programs were eradicating many of the hallmarks of internal colonialism.

Nevertheless, the legacy of internal colonialism affected the Welsh nationalist movement in three major areas. The earliest nationalist response was reaction to the devaluation of Welsh culture brought about by an internal colonial relationship that associated it with economic failure. Second, as internal colonies became candidates for regional development programs with the coming of the welfare state, nationalists tried to use such programs to increase Welsh economic unity and to secure a degree of self-determination for Wales. Their activities in this regard produced increased electoral support for the nationalist movement. Third, as some nationalist leaders became more aware of the persistent economic implications of an internal colonial past, and in particular of the impediments to developing a native capitalist base, they began to introduce socialist analysis into nationalist ideology.

Cultural Defense

An early example in Wales of the state elite blaming the economic disadvantages of an internal colony on its cultural distinctiveness was the 1847 Blue Books Report on Education in Wales. One of the commissioners who prepared the report explicitly attributed the fact that Welsh people did not fill the higher positions in the new industries to their use of the Welsh language (cf. G. Morgan, 1966, p. 50). Most of the nineteenth-century Welsh elite accepted this argument and attempted to improve the social status of the Welsh through measures designed to bring an English education to the children of Wales. Their leadership and example encouraged Welsh people to believe that acquisition of the English language and English culture was the key to economic betterment.

Thus, while at one level internal colonialism maintained cultural distinctions by reproducing them in the economic order, at another level it provided an incentive for individuals to change their identity to that of the majority culture in an attempt to improve their economic prospects. The collapse of the Welsh economy in the 1920s and 1930s produced both massive out-migration and, among those remaining behind, particularly in south Wales, a rapid decline in the use of the Welsh language, as parents, many speaking English only imperfectly, determined to use this language exclusively with their children in the hope of providing them with an escape from poverty.

Only a relatively few people were in positions in which the Welsh language and Welsh culture were of social and economic benefit to them, but these people made up a majority of the early membership of the Welsh Nationalist Party. Their main motivation for establishing a nationalist political party was to oppose the devaluation of Welsh culture and arrest its decline, and they showed little interest in economic issues. Saunders Lewis initially opposed developing specific economic policies, and the party's 1926 summer school did not include any formal discussion either of the General Strike of that year or of the subsequent prolonged miners' dispute (D. H. Davies, 1983, pp. 64–67). However, unlike the Cymru Fydd movement of the previous century, which was composed of Welsh politicians already enmeshed in a British political party, the Welsh Nationalist Party had been conceived as a separate Welsh political party. In their desire to break out of the British political mold, the leaders of the new party soon acknowledged that they should project a Welsh point of view, based on nationalist principles, in all major policy areas, including economics. The earliest economic position taken by the party was based on Saunders Lewis's vision of a society of small-property holders, in which both large capitalists and the 'rootless proletariat' would disappear. Only in such a society, he argued, could a vigorous national cultural life be sustained (D. H. Davies, 1983, pp. 85–86). This general concept was expanded by D. J. Davies, who was the party's principal spokesman on economics for several decades.[4] He argued from the perspective of guild socialism, asserting that the Welsh nation, as a community of communities, should encourage cooperative organizations of all types to limit the powers both of the state and of large capitalist firms (D. J. Davies, 1958, p. 61).

As the social and economic consequences of the depression began to undermine Welsh communities, nationalist leaders became more acutely aware of the links between economic reform and cultural survival. Saunders Lewis was much affected by the misery he encountered during a visit to the Rhondda in 1932. Writing in the *Welsh Nationalist* shortly afterwards, he accused the English government of creating "bestiality where there was once decency and civilised life." He went on to assert that the first priority of Welsh nationalism was "to change the entire system of government and of imperialist capitalism that has made my country the worst hell in Europe today." Nevertheless, the threat to Welsh culture, indeed the actual cultural devastation he had witnessed, rather than economic grievance, remained the driving force behind Lewis's nationalism.

The desirable revolution is that which will remove alien government from Wales and will re-create the Welsh nation and the Welsh "common tradition" as a necessary first step to the social and economic reconstruction of Wales and the swift overthrow of barbaric capitalist exploitation. [Quoted in D. H. Davies, 1983, p. 100]

While such long-term aspirations might have appealed to the Welsh electorate, the Welsh Nationalist Party did not have any significant electoral impact between 1925 and 1940. The character of its membership meant that the party gave little attention to conventional political activity. Most of the members regarded gatherings such as the annual summer school, which included academic lectures and various cultural events, as the most important party activity; party leaders were continually frustrated in their attempts to persuade members to participate in local politics. Only individuals already interested and involved in Welsh cultural life were likely to become active in the party; with the paucity of party electioneering, few others would have heard of it. For those who knew of its existence, a major drawback to its economic and social programs, aside from their utopian outlook, was that they offered no short-term suggestions to ameliorate the economic crisis but instead were predicated upon the attainment of self-government.

Economic Policies and Regional Development

At the end of the 1930s, the Welsh Nationalist Party published an essay that heralded a more realistic economic position. This essay, written by D. J. Davies and Noëlle Davies and entitled *Can Wales Afford Self-Government?*, confronted the objection that a self-governing Wales could not survive economically. The authors asserted that "Wales is poor because under an alien imperialist Government, seeking alien interests, her resources have been unused, disused and misused" (Davies & Davies, 1947, p. 36). They substantiated their claims with a review of specific government actions that led to the decline of the Welsh coal industry as well as with a critique of the transportation system. They concluded that a self-governing Wales, which would not have to spend large sums on defense or imperial affairs, would be able to raise adequate revenue through taxation, and would fully utilize Wales's natural resources to eliminate poverty.

The economic proposals in this essay were still utopian in their relevance only to a self-governing Wales. However, in its emphasis on economic planning for Wales as a whole, as well as in its detailed discussion of the problems of specific industries and of the economic infrastructure, the essay heralded a change in emphasis for the nationalist movement that gained momentum in the closing years of World War II. The early years of the war had been a period of confusion and decline for the Welsh Nationalist Party. The party had opposed conscription on the grounds that Welshmen should not be forced to fight in an English war, and this stance brought accusations of fascism. Many nationalists disagreed with the party's position, and both morale and membership suffered. However, at the close of the war and in the immediate postwar years, the Welsh Nationalist Party, by then increasingly referred to simply as Plaid Cymru, had an infusion of new members, and many branches that had become inactive during the early war years were reestablished (Butt Philip, 1975, pp. 22–24; D. H. Davies, 1983, pp. 223–251).

Many of these new members were returning servicemen whose sense of Welsh identity had been heightened by their years spent in the company of English soldiers and officers, who tended to identify them as Welsh regardless of whether or not they themselves were particularly conscious of being Welsh. Facing relatively open career choices on their return to civilian life and with a strengthened sense of Welsh identity, they were more likely to respond to the new nationalist message advocating economic planning for Wales and the establishment of Welsh economic units. These new members helped to redirect Plaid Cymru's electoral message, stressing intermediate goals rather than self-government and cultural survival. Such tactics had some success—the Blaid polled well, albeit under special postwar circumstances, in four by-elections in 1945 and 1946. The party's advocacy of Welsh divisions for newly nationalized industries may have attracted some voters who envisioned greater opportunities with increased numbers and proximity of managerial positions. However, the many workers in these industries who were already committed to career paths tied to their unions or to the Labour Party, both of which were British-based, clearly did not respond positively to this nationalist message.

The major structural factor prompting the transformation of the Blaid's political message was the growing involvement of the central state in economic life. The emphasis on economic planning for the postwar era provided an opportunity to establish Wales as a coherent economic unit. On the other hand, if government economic programs were not administered on an all-Wales basis, they posed a threat to Welsh political unification as well. Plaid Cymru argued for Wales to be treated as a unit in all of the new programs under consideration. The party was especially concerned to obtain a Welsh system for the generation and distribution of electricity. It was greatly impressed by the Tennessee Valley Authority project and by the ability of such an electrical service to transform the economic and social life of a region. As early as 1938, the Blaid had submitted a memorandum to the central government's electricity commissioners recommending that Welsh local authorities be allowed to set up a cooperative board to distribute electricity in Wales (Plaid Cymru, 1947, p. 7). This argument was repeated in the 1940s as it became apparent that nationalization was imminent. A pamphlet published by Plaid Cymru's London branch in 1944 called for setting up a Welsh electricity board and a Welsh Economic Commission, which between them could ensure coherent economic planning that would use electrification to stimulate industrial and agricultural development (Plaid Cymru, 1944; also cf. Plaid Cymru, 1943).

In addition to electricity, the Blaid made a similar case, also unsuccessfully,[5] for the coal and railway industries. In a pamphlet produced after the north and south Wales coal industries had been merged with separate British regional boards, it attacked the new structure, claiming that the Welsh coal industry would continue to be run by "gentlemen sitting in London" (D. J. Davies & Richards, 1948, p. 5). The gas industry was the only nationalized industry that treated Wales as a unit, and it provided the only example of the reinforcement of Welsh identity that the Blaid had hoped would result from establishing such Welsh economic units in all areas. The Wales Gas Board, which was created by the 1948 Gas Act, projected a strong Welsh image, publishing its reports bilingually and using the Welsh dragon as its symbol. The Welsh image of the board lessened considerably after the 1972 reorganization of the British gas industry, which replaced its federal structure with a more centralized one. [See Osmond (1974), pp. 51–74, for a detailed account of the reorganization and a critique of its effects.]

Besides arguing for the formation of Welsh organizations within government agencies and programs, the Blaid also advocated formation of a Wales Trades Union Council. A Plaid Cymru pamphlet that appeared at the end of the war contended that Welsh trade unionists suffered because the only organization tying together their various unions had its center outside Wales. "Because of that they cannot frame or further an industrial or economic policy affecting Welsh interests and life" (I. Davies, 1944, p. 2). The pamphlet was restrained in its references to the political objectives of Plaid Cymru and instead stressed the great contribution a unified Welsh working-class organization could make to furthering good international relations. Nevertheless, there was an indirect reference to the anticipated political consequences of a Wales TUC. "Such a Congress will ... reinforce the efforts Wales is now making to acquire for herself a measure of control over her destinies in particular spheres and eventually in all spheres" (I. Davies, 1944, p. 7). The Blaid was unsuccessful in this initiative. A TUC for Wales lay nearly thirty years in the future when other developments within the British bureaucracy would make it a more desirable institution for trade unionists who, for the most part, still would not be nationalists. In the 1940s, Welsh trade unionists perceived their interests in the political sphere to be best served by organization along British lines.

The Blaid's major rationale for Wales to be treated as a unit within the evolving government organizations and programs was "that the Welsh people are a nation, that their life as a nation cannot be split up into compartments, either in point of area or in point of economic function..." (Plaid Cymru, 1944, p. 11). Arguing their case based on Wales's historic identity was almost the only tactic available to nationalists at the time. The argument could not be based on administrative precedent, as the institutional structure differentiating Wales from England was extremely meagre. And there were other reasons for not respecting Welsh unity. Most planners who adopted a purely functional perspective advocated dividing Wales into several regions, attaching north Wales to Liverpool and mid-Wales to the English midlands. South Wales provided the strongest case of any Welsh region for treatment as an economic unit and even there some planners suggested its incorporation into a larger region based on Bristol (cf. Manners & Minchinton, 1964, p. 241).

In the final analysis, the early regional development programs did little to augment Welsh unity. Their main purpose was to reduce unemployment; they were specifically not intended to promote regional unity or independence (Conkling, 1964, p. 164). Nevertheless, so long as their ultimate form remained unresolved, Plaid Cymru continued to press its demand that Wales be treated as a unit under all the numerous nationalization schemes and planning programs that were put forward in the 1940s. However, this activity met with very limited success, and by 1950 the majority of these proposals had not been implemented.

The internal dynamism that had characterized Plaid Cymru in the late 1940s also began to disappear (Butt Philip, 1975, p. 80). The party had moved its central office from Caernarfon to Cardiff as a sign of its intent to represent the whole of Wales, not just the rural Welsh-speaking areas. However, most party leaders remained in the mold of Welsh-speaking cultural nationalists, united by a tight network of kinship and friendship. Many of the newer members, no longer motivated by the prospect of changing economic organization and not a part of the Blaid's social agenda, became inactive; others left the party, some to form another nationalist organization, the Welsh Republican Movement, whose main activity, for nearly a decade, was publication of an English-language newspaper.

Plaid Cymru fielded only seven candidates in the 1950 general election and did not improve its performance significantly over 1945. Another indication of a loss of direction was the heavy involvement of the party in the Parliament for Wales campaign. This campaign, which lasted from 1950 to 1956, was supported officially by the Liberal Party and also by a number of prominent Labour Party members. During the campaign Plaid Cymru stressed interparty cooperation to the extent of declaring, in 1951, that it would not oppose candidates of other political parties who supported Welsh home rule. The Parliament for Wales campaign thus absorbed the energies of nationalists and weakened Plaid Cymru's position as an autonomous political party (Butt Philip, 1975, pp.76, 82).

As judged by Plaid Cymru's electoral performance, political nationalism continued to decline through the 1966 general election. However, beginning in the early 1960s, the Blaid was gradually transformed from being a cultural organization with a political agenda into a genuine political party. This transformation culminated in a return to the emphasis on economic issues present in the late 1940s as well as in the development of a socialist position in nationalist ideology. One member described the main office of the Blaid before these changes took hold as having a "clubby atmosphere ... [It was] a small organization of the faithful centered on Caernarfon, sort of an enclave in Cardiff, and not a political party at all. The attitude was, who cares if you win or lose at an election; in fact, everyone expected to lose" (interview, 2 May 1977). But, during this period, disenchanted Plaid Cymru members, acting through external 'ginger groups,' were criticizing both the lack of professionalism and the undemocratic organization of the party hierarchy.[6] At the same time, the party was being transformed from below by increasing numbers of new members, mostly young, non-Welsh speaking, from the industrial areas of south Wales (Butt Philip, 1975, pp. 161–172; K. O. Morgan, 1972, p. 133). Most of them had benefitted from the higher education made available by the welfare state. Although coming from families and communities that were traditionally loyal to the Labour Party, they saw career prospects within their home areas limited by the British orientation of an entrenched Labour Party establishment, and many rejected Labour for what they regarded as its betrayal of socialism. One young man from Aberdare who joined the Blaid as a teenager in the mid-1960s explained:

My generation began to realize that all this tremendous loyalty to Labour had got us nowhere in our area and had got Wales nowhere as a whole. ... We suspected Labour not just on practical grounds, that they had not delivered on their promises, but also on ideological grounds that they were not a true socialist party .... We chose nationalism as the best way to pursue socialist ideals. [Interview, 9 February 1977]

By the 1970s, many of these individuals had become Plaid Cymru officers, national candidates, or staff members in the central office. But long before they attained formal positions of influence, they began to affect the party through their activity at grassroots level. Coming from areas with a tradition of effective local-level organization, they established and supported such grassroots organizations in their communities to maintain nationalist activity between elections. Much of what they accomplished was done without a great deal of direction from the central office. Furthermore, as one member of an early 1960s coordinating committee in the southeast commented, "We tended to dominate party conferences because we were so much more political in our orientation" (interview, 20 October 1976).

The first electoral success attendant upon the changing character of Plaid Cymru was the victory of Gwynfor Evans in a parliamentary by-election in Carmarthen on 14 July 1966, giving Welsh nationalism its first Member of Parliament. The new element in the Blaid's membership and among its supporters was even more clearly in evidence in its performance in two subsequent by-elections in southeast Wales constituencies. In Rhondda West in 1967 and Caerphilly in 1968, Plaid Cymru came a close second to Labour, attracting 40 percent of the total vote.

Another result of the Blaid's transformation was its development of a new economic policy, one with greater relevance for urban industrial areas. The policy was the product of a Research Group based in London and composed mainly of university graduate students. This group was formed in 1966, shortly after Gwynfor Evans's election to parliament, and although his victory was not the main impetus for its formation, it provided a research service for Evans, who found he did not receive much support from the central party organization in this regard. Research Group member Eurfyl ap Gwilym, who later became a Plaid Cymru chairman, described its composition and effect on the party:

The group formed in response to a need for professionalism that we felt existed in Plaid Cymru. ... There were thirty to forty people in the London Plaid Cymru group in the late 1960s, and maybe ten to fifteen of these were very active. But we have had a big effect on the party. Cymdeithas yr Iaith prospects tended to stay in Wales to go to university as a matter of principle. Also Cymdeithas appealed to those who wanted to take a more dramatic stance. ... They were not so keen on doing the hard political grind, which is what the Research Group did. ... The Research Group virtually ran the Rhondda by-election [in 1967] and then Phil Williams [a member of the group] was the candidate in Caerphilly [in the 1968 by-election]. [Interview, 16 March 1977]

Among the most active were those who wrote *An Economic Plan for Wales*, which appeared in 1970 and formed the basis of Plaid Cymru economic policy for nearly a decade. This document, which, it was generally recognized, was well researched and effectively argued, provided a plan for running the Welsh economy assuming a transfer of political control from London to Cardiff (Plaid Cymru, 1970, p. 1). However, it was also intended to be immediately useful to planners even without the attainment of full self-government (Plaid Cymru, 1970, p. 97).

The plan began with an assessment of the number of individuals who would need employment in Wales in 1976 and the number of jobs that would be available given the industrial base of the late 1960s, thereby arriving at an estimate of the number of additional jobs needed for each region in Wales. It then considered where growth should take place in order to meet the predicted shortfall of jobs. Admitting the necessity of selecting sites where growth was not only desirable but feasible, the plan broke with earlier Plaid Cymru policy and recognized the impossibility of stimulating growth evenly over the countryside (Plaid Cymru, 1970, pp. 37–38). Considering factors such as existing communication networks, availability of suitable industrial sites, climate, and potential for developing training facilities nearby, the plan selected nine centers where economic development should be concentrated. It then recommended specific types of industry for each region and, finally, suggested ways in which Wales's infrastructure, particularly its transportation facilities, could be improved to foster economic growth.

The plan envisaged roughly the same mix of public and private enterprise as was then in existence, not "an extreme socialist economy, with wholesale nationalisation . . ." (Plaid Cymru, 1970, p. 98). However, it proposed the creation of a National Development Authority with power to apply a program of increasing public involvement in industrial development so that "if private enterprise fails to respond [to standard techniques for encouraging regional development], the matter will not be left forgotten as is now the case but instead, public enterprise will undertake the work" (Plaid Cymru, 1970, p. 101). While the authors of the plan did not assume that a self-governing Wales could rely solely, or even primarily, on internal growth for its industrial development, they recommended greater control over international capital.

> The danger of outside capital is that control passes from Wales and to avoid this the capital sought must be, to some extent, a risk free investment (so that the risk control does not pass into the hands of those investing). What is envisaged is the launching by N.D.A. [the proposed National Development Authority] of a guaranteed interest fund. . . . [Plaid Cymru, 1970, p. 101]

Thus, although the plan was not a socialist program, it proposed a mechanism for government control and for direct government involvement that would move Wales in a socialist direction if standard development techniques proved inadequate.

In the 1960s, as in the 1940s, the major structural factor encouraging Plaid Cymru to develop detailed economic policies was the reappearance of regional development programs which carried with them the potential to establish Welsh economic structures. This potential, coupled with an effective nationalist response, produced Plaid Cymru's greatest political gains ever. The surge in nationalist support in the decade from 1966 to 1976 was both much greater and longer lasting than that of the immediate postwar years. The reason for the increased political potency of nationalist demands for Welsh economic organization was to be found in the multitude of other Welsh organizations that had been created in the intervening period in areas not directly related to the economy. Such a Welsh infrastructure gave credibility and a degree of official sanction to nationalist proposals that the Welsh economy be planned as a unit and that control over economic decisions be in Welsh hands.

In the late 1970s, the Labour government responded to a growing economic crisis by cutting back on government spending including reduction of funding or elimination of many measures for regional development. Nationalist electoral support also began to decline in this period and did not recover in the 1980s as successive Conservative governments pursued a policy of even more stringent cuts in government spending. Nevertheless, the body of Welsh organizations that had been created in the previous decades remained as a basis for Welsh distinctiveness, and Plaid Cymru retained its position as a viable, if frustrated, factor in Welsh politics.

A Socialist Direction

Another consequence of Plaid Cymru's commitment, beginning in the 1960s, to develop specific economic policies was that the party's ideological position began to move to the left. Nationalist analyses of the causes of Welsh economic problems sharpened awareness of the continued economic dependency in the relationship with England. Attempts to provide solutions stimulated formulation of increasingly socialist policies and led, in 1981, to the inclusion of a commitment to what was described as decentralized socialism in the party's basic goals.[7]

Plaid Cymru's move to the left was manifest in the content of motions and tone of the debates on economic issues at successive conferences beginning in the 1970s. The 1976 Annual Conference opened with two motions on housing, the first decrying the housing shortage in Wales and calling on Plaid Cymru councillors to fight for specific policies to provide adequate housing for the homeless. The proposer, fending off a motion to table, stressed the urgency of the situation and argued that Plaid Cymru, as "the only socialist party there is," must act. The motion passed but was followed by another on housing that proposed the sale of publicly owned houses to tenants under specified conditions. This motion was opposed by supporters of the first motion, who argued that it would make the plight of the homeless even worse and that the two motions were inconsistent. It was defeated by a large majority.

The move to the left was not entirely unopposed. The motion in the 1976 Conference that most clearly demonstrated cleavages within the Blaid on the question of its socialist direction was that on government economic policy. This motion noted various aspects of a growing economic crisis, primarily increasing unemployment and government expenditure cuts, accused the Labour government of deliberately creating unemployment to combat inflation, and concluded with specific demands that the government reverse its policy of expenditure cuts, end wage restraints, expand public sector industry, establish a minimum wage linked to inflation, and take other measures to reduce unemployment (Plaid Cymru, 1976, p. 26). Debate centered around two clauses which supported trade union action to force the government to reverse its economic policies and opposed wage restraint unequivocally. The delegation from Anglesey proposed that they be deleted, arguing that they "are regarded in Anglesey as making Plaid Cymru look like an extreme left-wing socialist party." The Anglesey amendment was defeated; however, another amendment considerably softened the opposition to wage restraint.[8]

By the mid-1970s, the socialist element of the party was fairly clearly in command, winning most debates. Yet their more extreme measures and voices were usually moderated. Perhaps the best example, in the 1976 Conference, of the sort of compromise economic position then being worked out was the Industrial Democracy motion, which was moved by Dafydd Wigley, Member of Parliament for Caernarfon and a former executive with the Hoover company in Merthyr Tydfil. The motion stated,

That Conference reiterates Plaid Cymru's fundamental policy in regard to industry that the Party resolutely opposes both capitalist control and exploitation of workers and centralised state control and reaffirms its belief in a third way in industry, based upon decentralisation and the co-operation of all the stockholders in an economic enterprise including employees, the providers of capital, the trade unions and the community within which the concern is rooted. [Plaid Cymru, 1976, p. 31]

The list of specific recommendations that followed included: extension of democratic principles to the workplace; acceptance of self-management by consent as the basic principle of industrial organization; vesting of ultimate control over a company in its employees; allowing the community in which an industry was located broad powers to influence policy decisions; and forbidding shareholders to receive more of the company's profits than employees. In spite of the motion's positive stance on workers' control, an

Toward a Welsh Economy

amendment was proposed that would have drastically altered its tone, turning it into a doctrinaire socialist declamation.[9] The proposer of this amendment argued, "There is no third way. There is only the socialist way or the capitalist way." This amendment was defeated and the original motion accepted. The main thrust of the arguments for the motion was illustrated by one appeal, made by a Merthyr Tydfil councillor, "not to play into the hands of the enemies of Plaid Cymru and of Wales who are trying to divide us between right and left. . . . The horizontal left–right axis of political choice is old hat; we must insist on the vertical axis from centralist to decentralist control." Although the motion's principal author and presenter, Dafydd Wigley, was regarded as representing a relatively conservative element within the party, the proposal was also supported by Dafydd Elis Thomas (MP, Merioneth), who was even then accepted as a bona fide socialist by the left both within and outside the Blaid. He supported the motion because "it is a Welsh answer, rather than Tory or Socialist, to the current crisis."

By 1980, with the deepening economic recession and rapidly escalating unemployment, the annual conference passed more radical motions on the economic situation with far less disagreement on their socialist wording than in 1976. A motion on the economic crisis asserted, "Conference believes that the economy of Wales has been devastated by (1) international capitalism (2) mismanagement by Westminster governments, Labour and Tory and (3) the failure to manage existing publicly-owned industries in the interests of the community" (Plaid Cymru, 1980, p. 17). Another motion, on Tory Unemployment Policy, deplored "the deliberate efforts of the present regime to turn Wales into an industrial desert" and attributed high unemployment to government policies, including "dogmatic antagonism towards public sector employment" (Plaid Cymru, 1980, p. 19).

The general leftist direction in Plaid Cymru policies during the previous decade was formally endorsed by the 1981 report of the Commission of Inquiry on the future of the party.

> [W]e are totally opposed to any form of capitalist exploitation, whether from inside or outside our borders. Any realistic evaluation of Plaid Cymru policy must conclude that it is socialist in nature—although the meaning we attach to the word may be totally different to that of many others who espouse it. We totally reject any form of government of a centralist type, which breeds bureaucracy, uniformity and intolerance. . . . Plaid Cymru's political stance would best be described as Decentralist Socialist. [Plaid Cymru, 1981b, p. 4]

The party's commitment to socialist principles was made more explicit by the 1981 Annual Conference. In a series of constitutional changes, Conference altered the party's three basic aims, to which all members were expected to subscribe, for the first time since 1931. The first aim of Plaid Cymru was changed from "self-government for Wales" to "a democratic Welsh socialist state." This change was reinforced in the second aim, which stated that Plaid Cymru members must strive to promote "the culture, language, traditions and the economic life of Wales," by adding the words "through the establishment of a decentalist socialist state" (Plaid Cymru, 1981a, pp. 1, 8, 28). The changes survived some dissension in the 1982 Annual Conference, when the term self-government was reincorporated into the first aim.[10] The support of the majority of party members for this socialist position was further affirmed by the 1984 election of Dafydd Elis Thomas (MP), a strong socialist, as Plaid Cymru president over Dafydd Iwan, who was associated with the more traditional section of the party.

The increasingly socialist position of Plaid Cymru was a target of criticism emanating both from members who felt it was not moving quickly enough as well as from those who resisted the leftward trend. On the one hand, shortly before the 1978 Annual Conference, a small but very vocal group calling itself the Welsh Socialist Republican Movement formed within the Blaid and began publishing its own newspaper, *Y Faner Goch* [The Red Flag]. The group's members were critical of what they felt to be insufficient commitment to socialist doctrine by Plaid Cymru, and they formally withdrew from the party in 1981. Their departure had little effect on the Blaid, whose leftward direction was essentially unaltered. The Welsh Republicans continued, for a brief period, to provide a mouthpiece for doctrinaire socialism within the nationalist movement from outside party ranks, and their literature was normally available at party gatherings. However, another group, the National Left, which numbered then Plaid Cymru vice-president Dafydd Elis Thomas among its members, coalesced within the Blaid filling any gap left by the Welsh Republicans. On the other hand, the 1982 Annual Conference witnessed the formation of a right-wing group, the Hydro Group, within Plaid Cymru. This group, which never gave evidence of consisting of more than a handful of adherents, specifically opposed the party's socialist position. However, although its presence was felt at several party conferences, it had little effect on party policy. The Hydro Group disbanded in 1986, responding in large measure to the decision of the 1985 Conference, which voted by a large majority to retain the party's socialist principles and policies (*Western Mail*, 15 July 1986).

By the 1980s, the disagreement within the Blaid was less that between socialist and conservative positions as between centralist and decentralist socialism. At a special meeting ("Back to 1926") during the 1980 Annual Conference, Dafydd Elis Thomas argued,

I support a strong Welsh state as the only way to plan, guarantee and control economic life—especially to control multinational capital. I am not a decentralist who believes communities can assume responsibility for themselves. [25 October 1980]

Phil Williams' minority report for the 1981 Commission of Inquiry also raised doubts about the practicality of the decentralist socialism advocated in the main report.[11] He argued that socialism and decentralism were not really harmonious, that a degree of compulsion was necessary to implement social equality, and that such compulsion must come from a central authority. Otherwise, how "can a prosperous community be used to enrich a poor community if it chooses not to? ... how do we ensure that the worker in a successful co-operative enterprise is equal to the worker in a co-operative enterprise that goes bankrupt?" (Plaid Cymru, 1981b, p. 111). Williams' proposed solution dealt less equivocally with a choice that had been broached by the main report[12] (cf. Plaid Cymru, 1981b, pp. 15–16).

If I can suggest one basic principle with which we can begin I would recommend that equality should always have priority, but whenever a function of government can be performed at a higher or lower level (if this does not disturb the basic equality of individuals and communities within society) it should always be performed at the lower level. In other words, we should combine as far as possible the greatest equality with the greatest degree of decentralism but when the two principles contradict it is to socialism that we should give our highest priority. [Plaid Cymru, 1981b, p. 111]

Thus, Plaid Cymru's commitment to socialism was growing from the 1970s, and by the early 1980s debate centered more on the form that socialism should assume in a Welsh state than on acceptance or rejection of socialist principles. Nevertheless, the party was not a doctrinaire socialist organization but rather a left-of-center political party which embraced socialist ideals. The development of these socialist policies, however, did not improve the party's electoral performance in the industrial areas of south Wales nor did they succeed in making an impression on trade unions, which remained closely wedded to the Labour Party establishment.

SUMMARY

The economic history of Wales as an internal colony affected the nationalist movement in three major areas. Initially, the emphasis placed on cultural defense reflected the nationalist attempt to revalue a culture whose denigration and decline was reinforced by its economic dependence. Subsequently, the introduction of regional development programs to alleviate some of the symptoms of such economic dependence provided an opportunity to increase popular support for the nationalist position. And, finally, the history of economic dependence encouraged the growth of socialist ideology within the nationalist movement. However, the electoral impact that the Blaid undoubtedly had, particularly in the decade from 1966 to 1976, owed much to factors other than the social and economic policies it propounded. Nationalism's position as a serious factor in Welsh political life was boosted by the recognition of Welsh unity implicit in the increasing organization of both state and independent institutions along Welsh lines, while the factors that facilitated the growth of such a Welsh infrastructure sprang primarily from the development of the welfare state in the postwar years.

NOTES

1. Neither did Welsh financial institutions prosper as industry expanded. The Cardiff Bank, established in 1806 and catering to local traders and gentry, closed in 1822 after its assets "became immobilized in the hands of London agents, as security for debts already outstanding with them" (Hodges, 1969a, p. 170). The Bank of England Branch Bank that was opened in Swansea in 1826 strengthened the connection of local bankers and traders with the London money market; and when it closed in 1859, the Bristol Branch was expected to assume its chief services to south Wales (R. O. Roberts, 1969, pp. 185-186). The savings banks that began to appear all across Wales early in the nineteenth century served a different clientele, the working class, and in the 1880s they were largely supplanted by the Post Office Savings Bank (Hodges, 1969b).

2. The Welsh rural areas, in the nineteenth century, produced a larger population than could be supported under the existing agricultural system. The resultant poverty and declining living standards drove the excess rural population to the relative prosperity offered by the newly developing industrial areas. However, when the industries in these areas went into decline beginning in the 1920s, there was no possibility that any significant proportion of their population could be reabsorbed by the rural areas.

3. Although there was some early industrial potential in north Wales, primarily copper mining and textiles, as well as iron-smelting on the smaller north Wales coalfield, these had all declined by about 1850 (Dodd, 1971, pp. 149-152; D. Williams, 1950, p. 219). Coal mining grew slowly but steadily in the area around Wrexham but was on a miniscule scale in comparison to south Wales. Between 1841 and 1911, the number of miners in Flintshire and Denbighshire grew from about 3,700 to 14,500; in south Wales, in the same period, the number went from 11,000 to 214,000. The most important industry in north Wales after 1850 was slate quarrying. This industry reached its peak in 1898 when it was employing nearly 17,000. It went into a steady decline thereafter and by the 1970s employed only a few hundred (Lindsay, 1974, pp. 253, 298).

4. D. J. Davies was a socialist who had supported the Independent Labour Party before becoming a nationalist (C. Thomas, 1958).

5. In the end, electricity was distributed through two agencies, one for north Wales combined with Merseyside and one for south Wales (Price, 1974, pp. 73–81).

6. As late as 1968, such criticism was still in evidence.

> With victory in its sights, the party leadership is afraid of division within the party. This has led to a fear of any kind of disagreement and by now to a fear of discussion. ... All important decisions are made by a few members of the establishment—or "court" as some members prefer, probably more accurately, to call it. The ordinary members, the branches, the District Committees, the National Council, even the Annual Conference itself are all kept out of the processes of decision-making. ... ["Welsh Nationalism, Plaid Cymru and fascism—does Plaid Cymru practice what it preaches?" *Cenedl Newydd/New Nation* (1 March 1968), p. 7]

The informal and personal style of operation that had characterized Plaid Cymru for decades was officially altered by the 1970 constitution, which established channels of access to policy making for individuals and branches and delineated areas of authority.

7. There had been attempts much earlier to force the party to adopt a socialist position. At the 1938 Conference a motion to abandon the existing economic policy in favor of one combining nationalism with socialist principles was put forth. But it was defeated, and the principle of cooperative democracy was reaffirmed (D. J. Davies, 1949, p. 16; D. H. Davies, 1983, pp. 94–95).

8. The amended version said that wage restraint "in itself is not a solution to inflation, and unless combined with other measures will merely result in a sharp fall in the living standards of the people of Wales without creating any prospect of economic prosperity in the future" (Plaid Cymru, 1976, p. 26).

9. The proposed amendment would have deleted everything in the motion beginning with the phrase "and reaffirms its belief in a third way" and replaced it with the following.

> However, Conference recognises that to end capitalist control would be a revolutionary step, changing the whole basis of society.
>
> Conference has no illusions that the onwers [sic] and controllers of capital, and all those who have a vested interest in the perpetuation of private and state capitalism, would acquiesce in the dismantling of their system.
>
> Therefore, Conference appreciates the need for a radical socialist movement to organize and undertake the abolition of capitalism, as far as possible through peaceful and democratic means—and recognises that the Labour Party cannot fulfill that role.
>
> A new society in Wales—based on workers' control and social onwership [sic] of industry, and organized for the benefit of local and national communities, can only be achieved once the grip of international finance and capital on western Europe has been broken [Plaid Cymru, 1976, p. 34].

10. The exact wording became "to secure Self Government for Wales through the establishment of a democratic socialist state" (Plaid Cymru, 1982, p. 30); the wording of the second aim became "to safeguard and promote the culture, language, traditions, environment and the economic life of Wales through the establishment of a decentralist socialist state."

11. The author of the minority report, Phil Williams, had nearly captured the Caerphilly constituency in a by-election in 1968. He was also a former party chairman and was elected Plaid Cymru vice-president in 1982.

12. In considering how to define the powers of the central state under decentralist socialism, the main report asserted that the role of the state had to be considered in light of "the need to act as a co-ordinator and arbitrator between the interests of the various diverse communities at local level . . ." and "the need to ensure an acceptable sysem of resource equalisation between regions of significantly different levels of prosperity . . ." (Plaid Cymru, 1981b, p. 15).

5

Rise and Decline with the Welfare State

The central British state was the primary external factor influencing Welsh nationalism from the nineteenth century onwards. A relatively high level of state involvement in religion combined with a vital Welsh nonconformist tradition to make religious issues central to nineteenth-century nationalism. Electoral reform provided the means and legislative activity the medium through which these early nationalists pursued their goals. The state bureaucracy expanded gradually in the opening decades of the twentieth century, and, although a quasi-independent political nationalism had disappeared with Cymru Fydd in the 1890s, the heritage of special legislation for Wales and the residual nationalism of the Liberal Party were sufficient to secure the establishment of Welsh departments in a few of the new or enlarged state bureaucratic agencies. In the 1920s and 1930s, the Liberal Party, along with its brand of romantic nationalism, proved ineffectual in the face of severe economic depression, and the Labour Party effectively displaced the Liberals in Welsh politics. The new independent Welsh Nationalist Party (Plaid Genedlaethol Cymru), which arose in this same period, projected a very different nationalist image: instead of the former Liberal nationalists' eagerness to secure a place for Welsh culture within the British imperial tradition, the new party sought positive valuation for a separate Welsh cultural tradition, to be supported by Welsh political institutions. Although the party developed an independent nationalist position in most policy areas and attracted a small core of activists, it received little popular support until after World War II.

However, the growth of the welfare system in the postwar era represented a major qualitative change in the nature of the British state and brought in its wake a serious challenge and new opportunities for nationalists.

The welfare state weakened community institutions as it assumed many of their responsibilities, and it also greatly increased the frequency of contact between individuals and the state. Such processes of centralization and standardization along British lines imperiled maintenance of a minority cultural identity. In order to protect Welsh identity, nationalists had to win recognition for Welsh unity and distinctiveness within the evolving state bureaucracy. They argued for separate provisions for Wales within all the new or expanded state agencies and programs, basing their case both on Wales's cultural distinctiveness and on administrative precedent. The latter argument proved increasingly effective, following the creation of a number of Welsh organizations, as a result of which it became acceptable even to many of those hostile to nationalism. The creation of the Welsh Office in 1964 was a major breakthrough in this process as it encouraged the growth of a Welsh infrastructure both inside and outside the bureaucracy. Of particular importance among external organizations created to deal with the bureaucracy were those representing the interests of business and of labor—the Welsh office of the Confederation of British Industry (CBI), and the Wales Trades Union Council (TUC). Both of these organizations were formed to enable these interests to deal directly with the Welsh Office.

The many Welsh organizations created in the decades after World War II in areas as dissimilar as agriculture and the arts bolstered Welsh identity by giving it official recognition. In addition, the Welsh dimension of particular issues received more attention than it would have under a completely centralized British administration. Nowhere was this more evident than in the role of the Welsh Water Authority in the long-standing controversy over English use of Welsh water resources. Furthermore, the Welsh bureaucracy, particularly the Welsh Office, provided a more readily assailable target for nationalist campaigns than did a more remote London-based administration. Finally, the existence of a large number of Welsh organizations, most of which were nonpartisan and very few of which were to any degree pronationalist, helped build a broader base of support for a degree of political as well as administrative autonomy for Wales, as was illustrated by the Wales TUC's support for a Welsh Assembly. Beginning in the late 1970s, the intrusion of another external bureaucracy, that of the European Economic Community, stimulated a similar process, of creating new Welsh organizations or bolstering the autonomy of existing ones, to that which had occurred with the growth of the British bureaucracy.

THE WELFARE STATE AND COMMUNITY INSTITUTIONS

While the history of welfare legislation in Britain can be traced to the sixteenth century, World War II marked a decisive break in the extent and form of central government involvement in the lives of individual citizens (Bruce, 1968; Fraser, 1973). The experiences of total war were a major impetus behind the postwar transformation of an uncoordinated, locally administered collection of social programs into the welfare state. The two pillars of the welfare state were the social security system and the national health service, both of which came into effect in 1948. In addition, the government's postwar commitment to full employment resulted in the creation of regional development schemes and in the nationalization, during the 1940s, of most basic industries.

The massive involvement of the central government in social and economic life and the consequent changes in life styles after World War II greatly reduced the importance of community organizations. The role of local government became an increasingly dependent one, with the central government providing the bulk of its finance and influencing many of the decisions regarding allocation. Aside from local government, the most important community organizations in Wales were the chapels, in rural areas, and the local lodges of the National Union of Mineworkers (NUM), in the industrial valleys. After World War II, however, the importance of the chapels as centers of social life was substantially diminished by the assumption of responsibility by the state for social welfare, access to mass media, and greater availability of public and private transport. Similarly, in industrial areas, economic diversification and nationalization of the coal industry brought about a decline in the social role of the NUM. Prior to World War II, the NUM had been the major social and political organization in the valleys (cf. Pelling, 1965, pp. 125–132). One resident described its former importance:

Life in the valleys revolved completely around the union. The Lodge [the NUM local] was the only source of power or protection against the owners. It permeated the society with its Women's Committee and Welfare Committee; the pit even financed the local library and it provided recreation and so forth. It was really a mini-welfare state within the community. [Interview, 9 February 1977]

Several factors contributed to the breakdown of this unitary community structure. First, with industrial diversification, the NUM ceased to be the only major union in the region. Second, the closure of many mines in the 1960s and the resulting transfer of miners meant that many no longer worked in their home communities. Finally, the transfer of responsibility for social welfare to the state removed an important union function. Thus, the centrality of the lodge in community social life disappeared. The importance of the NUM in the political organization of the region also lessened, primarily as a result of nationalization, which brought a degree of cooption of the union by government/management, particularly when the Labour Party was in power.

Thus, the growth of the welfare state had the effect, in industrial as well as rural parts of Wales, of lessening the importance of community social and political organizations in favor of individualistic ties with the central state bureaucracy. At the same time, as the bureaucracy grew, access to centers of power became increasingly difficult. Few individuals had the time, personal connections, or technical knowledge required to deal successfully with the bureaucracy in all the areas in which it affected their lives. Thus, the expansion of the welfare state unintentionally created a role for new intermediate-level organizations which could assume some of the burden of representing individual and group interests within the bureaucracy. Such organizations appeared throughout Britain, representing a variety of special interests. In Wales, most of them found it advantageous to claim a particular Welsh interest group as their natural constituency and hence to organize on a Welsh base. The major reason for the efficacy of the Welsh dimension in such organizations was that a Welsh infrastructure was simultaneously being created within the state bureaucracy itself. The most influential of the Welsh organizations in this regard was the Welsh Office.

THE WELSH OFFICE

Nineteenth-century nationalists had advocated, with varying degrees of enthusiasm, the establishment of national institutions in Wales. Their most ambitious proposal was the 1892 National Institutions (Wales) Bill to create a Welsh secretary of state. Although backed by seventeen Welsh MPs, the bill was dropped when several influential Welsh Liberals refused to support it (K. O. Morgan, 1963, pp. 109–110). The first real advances in the devolution of administrative powers to Wales were made in the decade prior to World War I, when separate Welsh departments were established in education (1907) and agriculture (1912).[1] It was fortuitous for the eventual growth of a Welsh infrastructure that the earliest expansion of the British bureaucracy took place in sectors where arguments for special treatment for Wales were strong. In both education and agriculture, Wales had particular problems not common to Britain as a whole, and these provided the justification for separate departments (Randall, 1972, pp. 354–357).

No significant additional administrative devolution took place until the period of great bureaucratic growth following World War II. With the increasing administrative complexities of the new welfare programs, many government departments were reorganized on a regional basis. In most cases Wales was treated as an administrative unit, and when a new Ministry of Housing and Local Government was created in 1951, it had a separate Welsh Office. In addition, a Council for Wales had been established in 1948 to advise the government on the impact of its policies in Wales.

As the number of Welsh administrative units accumulated, arguments intensified favoring a secretary of state to provide some coherence to the administrative system in Wales. Nevertheless, successive governments chose instead to respond with largely symbolic gestures such as the inauguration of a Welsh Day in Parliament and the creation of the post of Minister for Welsh Affairs.[2] Pressure continued to mount through the 1950s for some form of devolution of powers to Wales. An interparty campaign calling for a Parliament for Wales was organized in 1950 and, in 1956, presented a petition carrying over 250,000 signatures to Parliament.[3] The strongest pressure for a secretary of state for Wales came from the advisory Council for Wales, which, in 1957, brought in detailed proposals for the creation of a Welsh Office modeled on the Scottish Office. When this proposal was turned down by the Conservative government, the council's chairman and trade-union leader, Huw T. Edwards, resigned the chairmanship and subsequently underlined his protest by leaving the Labour Party for Plaid Cymru. Within the Labour Party itself, there was considerable opposition to the idea of a Welsh secretary. But Labour deputy-leader and Llanelli MP James Griffiths strongly favored the idea and managed to persuade the party's policy-making committee to include it in their manifestos for 1959 and 1964. As a result of his efforts, Griffiths was appointed the first Welsh secretary when Labour was returned to power in 1964 (K. O. Morgan, 1982, pp. 332–333, 380–381; Osmond, 1977, pp. 100–103).

While the need for administrative reorganization was a major argument for a Welsh secretary of state, the Labour government initially stressed that the position was created primarily out of respect for Welsh national sentiment and as a recognition of Welsh nationhood. This reflected Labour's intention to limit the office to a symbolic role, confining the secretary's powers to general oversight of government policies in Wales. However, once established, the office began gradually to aggrandize power (Randall, 1972).

The secretary's first executive powers, which dated from the formation of the Welsh Office, were over housing and roads. In 1969, during a central reorganization that combined the areas of health and social security, the Welsh Office managed to acquire executive responsibility for health, but not social security, in Wales. In the same year, the Welsh Office also acquired some responsibility for agriculture, achieving representation on the annual price review boards, but not full executive power; it gained complete control over the Ministry of Agriculture in Wales in 1977. Responsibility over primary and secondary, but not higher, education was acquired in 1970. Over the years, the office also accumulated executive functions in a variety of other areas such as water, forestry, and tourism. In addition, the Welsh Office had oversight power of other government departments in Wales and thereby gained some control over the execution of government industrial policies and over economic planning in Wales (Rowlands, 1972, pp. 334–337).

While the Welsh Office generally represented special Welsh issues more effectively in the central administration than did the ministers of the functional departments concerned, it had little influence on policy making (Rowlands, 1972, pp. 340–343). Nevertheless, the Welsh Office was the major factor in augmenting the Welsh infrastructure, both by establishing control over executive powers formerly exercised by the central bureaucracy and by stimulating the creation of other Welsh organizations. Such stimulus was responsible, for example, for the establishment of a Welsh regional office of the CBI. The Welsh branch was one of ten regional offices of the CBI and was quite small in comparison to the others. Its relative autonomy in this highly centralized organization was explained by its Research Officer:

A branch like Bristol just looks after the needs of its members in the area and all lobbying is done in London. In the Cardiff branch we have a large degree of contact with government ourselves ... and therefore the CBI branch in Wales is semi-autonomous. [Interview, 25 April 1977]

In addition, as the Welsh Office extended its responsibilities, it provided another argument for the devolution of political power to Wales, namely, that the growing mass of nominated agencies under its control, numbering 75 by 1977, should be made more directly accountable to the electorate (cf. Osmond, 1977, pp. 38–39).

THE WALES TRADES UNION COUNCIL

The Welsh Office also played a major role in stimulating the formation of the Wales Trades Union Council, arguably the most important of the numerous Welsh organizations created to deal with the British bureaucracy after World War II. While Plaid Cymru had advocated the creation of such an organization since the immediate postwar years, the Wales TUC did not come about as a result of nationalist pressure. In fact, Phil Williams, party chairman in 1976, recalled that "active campaigning for a Wales TUC was soft-pedalled by Plaid Cymru during the period when the Wales TUC was actually being formed in order to improve the chances of its being established" (interview, 20 October 1976).

Prior to the formation of the Wales TUC, Welsh union organization consisted of North and South Wales Regonal Advisory Committees to the British TUC. The idea of a Wales TUC surfaced occasionally in various unions in Wales in the 1950s and 1960s.[4] The most important convert to the idea in this period was the south Wales branch of the NUM, whose support from 1966 onwards had been stimulated by the establishment of the Welsh Office. The regional committees perceived any such body as a threat to their interests and resisted the idea, arguing that Wales was not an economic unit and hence that there was no commonality of interest between union members in north and south Wales. Furthermore, they argued, most unions administered Wales in three sections, usually with north and mid-Wales attached to separate English regions. However, beginning in 1968, the Transport and General Workers Union (TGWU) undertook a reorganization of its separate north and south Wales branches into a single Welsh regional structure. The main reason for the reorganization was to provide a stronger financial base for a full-time secretary. Nevertheless, once so organized and under its new leader, George Wright, the TGWU began to press for a Wales TUC, and despite opposition from the British TUC it joined the NUM to establish such a body. An organizational meeting was held in 1972, and a constitution was adopted at a conference in 1973. The central TUC was thus presented with a fait accompli and gave its approval to the Wales TUC prior to the 1974 conference (Osmond, 1977, pp. 116–121). The Research Officer for the Wales TUC described the process of winning British TUC approval:

At the time of the formation of the Wales TUC, there were already regional councils in Wales as part of the British TUC. So initially they resisted the formation of a stronger Wales TUC. They feared separatism as a result in the first place. Secondly, the vested interests of those on the regional councils meant that they opposed their own dissolution. And finally they were afraid that a Wales TUC would become a platform for Plaid Cymru. ... George Wright was able to overcome these objections by pointing out first that there would have to be close links with the British TUC, because the Wales TUC would depend on them for funding. Also, the old regional councils' leadership was essentially absorbed into the new Wales TUC structure. ... Wright also knew that the TGWU would be the power union in the Wales TUC, and he knew that it politically did not reflect Plaid Cymru so he could assure the British TUC on that score. [Interview, 18 March 1977]

In spite of its organizers' determination that the Wales TUC should not reflect nationalist aspirations, the heightened nationalist sentiment of the late 1960s had played a part of its creation. A document drawn up by the British TUC, in response to the 1973 conference of the Wales TUC, noted that, whereas the argument against a Wales TUC based on the lack of economic unity in Wales had been relevant in the 1950s and 1960s,

> recent events imply that this view had to be modified. The resurgence of interest in Welsh nationhood and in Welsh culture which is reflected in the actions of the Government in treating Wales as a separate entity—particularly by the establishment of a Welsh Office and a Secretary of State for Wales—mean that the case for establishing an all-Wales trade union is considerably strengthened. [Quoted in Osmond, 1977, pp. 121–122]

An additional consideration was that the labor movement's rival organization, the CBI, had already set up a Welsh section that dealt directly with the Welsh Office. Thus, the Wales TUC was established as a result of the growth in importance of the Welsh bureaucracy linked to the Welsh Office, which was in itself a response to general nationalist advances though not to direct nationalist pressure.

Although Plaid Cymru had very little representation on the Wales TUC, claiming only twelve Plaid members as delegates at the 1977 conference and no party members on the General Council, the Blaid was able to link itself with the new Welsh body, in joint opposition to the Labour government, during the 1975 campaign against continued British membership in the EEC. Although the referendum resulted in a large majority in favor of continued EEC membership, Plaid Cymru emerged with increased credibility, having enjoyed considerable public exposure during the campaign sharing a platform with leading trade unionists (Balsom & Madgwick, 1978).

In spite of its anti-nationalist position, the Wales TUC added its voice to those advocating devolution of political power to Wales. At its 1977 conference, it affirmed its support for a Welsh Assembly with legislative power (*Western Mail*, 23 April 1977). During the referendum campaign, the Wales TUC modified its demand for a legislative assembly to bring it into line with the government's devolution bill, which only provided executive powers for the proposed Welsh Assembly. However, the devolution proposals were openly regarded by the Wales TUC leadership as only a first step. The general secretary, George Wright, stated that the reason for moderating their position was simply to secure a larger 'yes' vote: "We are keen to get an Assembly under way as something we can build on," he said (quoted in *Western Mail*, 16 April, 1978). After the defeat in the referendum, the Wales TUC returned to its original position favoring a Welsh Assembly with far broader powers than the government had offered.

POLITICAL DEVOLUTION AND A WELSH ASSEMBLY

Pressures from the growing Welsh infrastructure and the increased electoral appeal of Welsh and Scottish nationalism both contributed to the political atmosphere that led Labour to develop its devolution proposals. The process began in 1968, when the Labour government appointed a commission on the constitution to examine the question of Scottish and Welsh home rule. The resulting report of the Kilbrandon Commission, which appeared in 1973, recommended unanimously that Wales and Scotland be given elected assemblies, and a majority of the Commission's members also advocated that these assemblies have legislative powers and considerable fiscal freedom. The Labour Party, by then no longer the party of government, balked at granting legislative power to a Welsh Assembly but approved the concept of an elected assembly with executive responsibilities. The February 1974 election, which brought Labour back to power, also produced significant nationalist advances, particularly in Scotland, putting the government under pressure to act on the Kilbrandon Commission Report. The devolution bill that the government brought out in 1976 followed closely the Labour Party's original reaction to the Kilbrandon Report, proposing elected assemblies for Wales and Scotland but differentiating between them in that the Welsh Assembly was to have only executive functions, whereas the Scottish Assembly was to be granted legislative powers.

The bill had a difficult passage through the various parliamentary stages leading toward a final vote. A major source of the government's problems was the opposition to it from within the ranks of the Labour group of MPs.[5] Opponents of the measure secured amendments requiring that the proposed assemblies be submitted to referenda in Scotland and Wales and that they receive the support of 40 percent of the total electorate before being given final parliamentary approval. The government's acceptance of the referendum amendment went against the wishes of the Welsh Labour Party. Shortly after the referendum their research officer claimed,

As a party we had never argued the case for a Welsh Assembly on the basis that the Welsh people were demanding it. Rather we felt that the proposals would improve democracy in Wales. We were opposed, as a party, to a referendum, and we advised the government to allow the bill to be defeated in parliament rather than accept a referendum. [Interview, 7 March 1979]

In the event, the referenda, held on 1 March 1979, resulted in a resounding defeat for the proposed assembly in Wales, where only 20 percent voted in favor, and a narrow victory in Scotland, where 52 percent (only 33 percent of the total electorate, however) voted in favor. Two months after the referenda, the Labour government was defeated in a general election, which also produced severe nationalist losses, especially in Scotland, and the proposed Scottish and Welsh Assemblies became a dead issue.

The referenda took place against a background of serious economic problems in Britain, problems that had already forced the Labour government to initiate cutbacks in government services and spending. Many voters had begun to perceive the cost of large government as outweighing the benefits, and arguments that portrayed the proposed Assembly as just one more costly tier of government proved damaging. The election of a Conservative government the following May on a platform promising even more substantial cuts in government spending and a significant reduction of the government's role in the economy was a further reflection of this political climate.

The results in the referendum were also influenced by relations within and among the various organizations involved in the campaign. The major organizations supporting the Labour government's proposed Assembly for Wales were: the Wales TUC; a nonpartisan organization calling itself the Wales-for-the-Assembly Campaign; and Plaid Cymru. The only major organization opposing the assembly, besides the Conservative Party, was the nonpartisan No-to-the-Assembly Campaign. Given the Labour-dominated, predominantly working-class political composition of south Wales in particular, a relatively easy victory in the referendum should have been possible simply on the basis of Labour Party and Wales TUC support. However, these organizations essentially confined their support to formal endorsements; neither the Wales TUC nor the Labour Party put their full resources into grassroots campaigning. Plaid Cymru actually organized and carried out much of the door-to-door distribution of literature from all sources, including Labour Party and TUC leaflets. A TUC official explained the relationship among the various pro-Assembly organizations:

Actually the Labour Party organization is mostly in control of the other organization [Wales-for-the-Assembly Campaign], at least at the upper level. At the grassroots level, actually pushing literature through letter boxes, it tends to be Plaid. [Interview, 14 February 1979]

The failure of the Labour Party to organize significant support at the community level was cited by the Welsh Labour Party's research officer as a major reason for their defeat in the referendum. "People got leaflets with [then Labour prime minister] Callaghan's picture but they would still ask, 'Where are our local councillors?'" (interview, 7 March 1979).

Nor was such lack of discipline among Labour Party members confined to local politicians. Many Labour MPs feared that any degree of autonomy for Wales and Scotland, where the party's voting strength lay, would mean a loss of power at the center of British politics, and some Welsh MPs whose political ambitions lay outside Wales openly opposed their own party's devolution proposal. Thus, opposition within the Labour Party to the assembly proposals was led by six Welsh Labour MPs, prominent among them being Neil Kinnock, who would become leader of the Labour Party in 1983. This group contended that the Assembly was a "sellout to nationalism" and would be a first step onto the "slippery slope of separatism." They argued that the Assembly would have no power to improve the economic climate in Wales, stressing that it "could not get an extra hospital bed, a mile of motorway, or a classroom" (*Western Mail*, 25 January 1979). Finally, they suggested that the Assembly would siphon both money and power from local government. Kinnock claimed that the Assembly would cause local authorities in Wales to lose one million pounds a year and asked, "Who is prepared to give up £1m. to be bossed by an institution in Cardiff?" (quoted in *Western Mail*, 7 February 1979). Presenting the Assembly as a threat to local government enabled the anti-Assembly group to win the local Labour Party councillors to their side with relative ease.

The pro-Assembly organization responded to these attacks with a series of academic essays setting forth reasons for supporting a Welsh Assembly. At a press conference to publicize the release of one such paper on the contributions an Assembly could make to the Welsh economy, their spokesman offered little more than the conviction that it would provide a more "adventurous attitude" and "buccaneering spirit" in the search for new industry and jobs for Wales (31 January 1979).

While the referendum vote was a defeat for Labour Party policy, it also indicated that the nationalist movement in Wales had entered a period of decline following its advances in the late 1960s and early 1970s. This decline was further verified by the results of the general election held in May of 1979 when Gwynfor Evans lost his Carmarthen seat, reducing Plaid Cymru's parliamentary representation to two. The financial burdens of these two campaigns left the Blaid able to retain only a skeleton staff of two full-time employees in the central office. And many party members began to doubt the possibility of achieving nationalist goals through the electoral process and to ask what direction party campaigning could profitably take in the future.

The main reason Plaid Cymru was hit so hard by the referendum loss was the extent of its involvement in the campaign. Early in February 1979, Gwynfor Evans had let it be known that "until the referendum on March 1 his priorities will not be at the House of Commons but sharpening the party's organization for a majority 'yes' vote" (*Western Mail*, 2 February 1979). And the party made a major effort to provide workers for grassroots activity, such as literature distribution. However, Plaid Cymru's commitment to the devolution proposals had only reached this level in the four months prior to the referendum. When the measure was first aired by the Labour Party, in 1973, the Plaid Cymru Annual Conference passed a resolution approving, for the first time, an elected Welsh Assembly even without full sovereignty but stipulated that any such assembly should have legislative power and full control over economic affairs (*Western Mail*, 29 October 1973). Enthusiasm for the Assembly waned markedly following the introduction of the government's legislation, and the 1976 Annual Conference reaffirmed the party's commitment to full national status for Wales, with devolution mentioned only obliquely (Plaid Cymru, 1976, p. 20). During the following two years, Plaid Cymru continued to have difficulty determining what tactical position it should assume on the devolution proposals.[6] The question was finally resolved, after vigorous debate, by the 1978 Annual Conference, which voted to support the Labour Party's proposals and officially urged members to work for a 'yes' vote in the referendum (Plaid Cymru, 1978, p. 23). Thus, although a minority in the party continued to oppose the Assembly, Plaid Cymru marshalled a great deal of active support for the campaign in the months before the referendum, and the defeat was a major setback for party morale. Indeed, the failure of the Labour Party to discipline its rebel MPs led some in the Blaid to claim that the entire devolution issue was developed by Labour solely to discredit nationalism (cf. Plaid Cymru, 1981b, p. 97).

Although hopes for political devolution were dashed in the referendum, administrative devolution went on apace and was largely unopposed. Even in the middle of the referendum campaign, the publicity officer of the No-to-the-Assembly Campaign said that their supporters "believe that devolution is an 'on-thing' in Wales" (interview, 7 February 1979). And after the referendum, those who supported the Assembly continued to argue that the need for democratic control over the growing Welsh bureaucracy was not diminished and was, in fact, becoming more pressing. Significantly, the Wales TUC returned to its original advocacy of a Welsh Assembly with legislative and taxation powers.

THE WELSH WATER AUTHORITY

In addition to giving official recognition to Welsh identity and strengthening the argument for a degree of Welsh political autonomy, the Welsh bureaucracy sometimes increased public awareness of the Welsh dimension of specific issues. Such a process occurred in the 1970s regarding the question of control over Welsh water resources. Water had been an emotional issue in Welsh politics for over two decades. In 1957 the English city of Liverpool won parliamentary approval to flood the Welsh valley of Tryweryn, forming a reservoir to augment the city's water supply. This action, which destroyed the Welsh-speaking community of Capel Celyn, was approved over the opposition of 27 Welsh MPs and in spite of Welsh public opinion against the measure (Butt Philip, 1975, pp. 77, 297). Tryweryn became one of the most evocative incidents in the nationalist movement, embodying as it did the indifference of the English government to Welsh cultural values. However, the issue made little impact among non-Welsh speakers. The establishment of the Welsh National Water Development Authority in 1974[7] brought a new dimension to the controversy over Welsh water, making it relevant to both Welsh and non-Welsh speakers in virtually all parts of Wales. In essence, the existence of the Welsh Water Authority enabled nationalists to link the issues of cultural deterioration and economic exploitation.

Water services in England and Wales were reorganized by the 1973 Water Act, which replaced a multitude of local organizations with nine regional authorities in England and one in Wales. The boundary of the Welsh Water Authority was a mixture of functional considerations and recognition of Welsh territorial integrity. It did not follow the Wales–England border exactly, because regional areas were supposed to be based on natural catchment areas, and thus a large portion of mid-Wales was included in the English Severn-Trent Authority. Nevertheless, north and south Wales, which did not belong to the same river system, were contained within the single Welsh authority, because, according to the public relations officer for the authority, "The district is ethnically and geographically distinct, like Scotland, and the suggestion to split it would have been politically inadvisable. Wales is a proud nation" (interview, 9 June 1977).

Changes effected by the 1973 Water Act caused regional inequities in water charges to be more readily discernible. They revealed that, in addition to supplying water for large areas of England, Wales was paying more for its water than were most English regions. The disparities had not been so obvious prior to reorganization primarily because the central government had allowed much of the extra cost to be made up by the general rate funds of local authorities, rather than by direct water charges to the consumer. Reorganization eliminated this practice, whereupon water rates in Wales jumped by more than 50 percent in one year.

The principal reason given for the higher cost of water in most parts of Wales was the greater expense of supplying it to what were predominantly rural areas; urbanized southeast Wales would have remained relatively untouched by the water issue but for the effect of the Water Charges Equalisation Bill. This bill, which was implemented by the Welsh Water Authority beginning in 1975, required that water charges be equalized within each authority. Its immediate effect was a sharp jump in water rates in most urban areas in Wales, thus involving southeast Wales directly in the water issue for the first time (Broady, 1977). In essence, the bill ensured that all parts of Wales would be seen as equally disadvantaged vis-à-vis the English regions. The feeling developed, even within the authority itself, that if equalization was a valid principle within an authority, it should also be applied between regions.

The Welsh National Water Development Authority may not have gone on record claiming that its finances deserve special consideration; but it does admit that it has the highest water charges of the ten regional water authorities and that it would like to bring its charges into line with its neighbours by levying extra charges on water exported to other water authorities.[8] [Welsh National Water Development Authority, 1975, p. 1]

Plaid Cymru's initial involvement in the water issue was its opposition to the drowning of Welsh valleys for the benefit of English cities. The issue was treated in party publications primarily as a cultural concern (cf. Evans, 1956). However, with the establishment of the Welsh Water Authority, the water issue became at once more clearly related to economic questions and of more universal concern. From the first announcement in February 1974 of increased water rates, Plaid Cymru began to approach the water issue as another example of English exploitation of Welsh resources. The Blaid argued that water resources should be used to further the well-being of the people of Wales. The motion on water at the 1976 Annual Conference called for "the formation of a Welsh Water Board which would control all Welsh water." In addition, the board "would be responsible for selling Welsh water to other parts of Britain by negotiation" (Plaid Cymru, 1976, pp. 4–5). The argument for treating water as a national resource had been bolstered by the effects of a serious drought in the summer of 1976. In southeast Wales, water rationing was enforced, with supplies being cut off up to seventeen hours a day, while no restrictions were placed on water usage in the English midlands, whose water came from reservoirs in mid-Wales. Although this particular issue lost force once the immediate water shortage ended, the matter of unequal water rates between Wales and England remained controversial. When the Conservative government which came to power in 1979 declared its intention to cancel plans for equalization of water charges between authorities at a time when water rates in Wales were rising rapidly, the issue came to the fore again. Plaid Cymru launched a very widely supported campaign to refuse payment of water bills until the Welsh Water Authority was allowed to negotiate a fairer return for water sold to English authorities. The water-rates campaign ended early in 1983, when Plaid leadership reached an agreement with the Welsh Water Authority to pursue the controversy through the courts.

Thus the existence of the Welsh Water Authority defined a Welsh dimension to a particular problem, broadened the public for whom the problem was relevant, and provided a target for nationalist-led protest. At the same time, the authority attempted to increase its own autonomy, thereby transferring a degree of decision-making power from the British center to Wales.

THE WELSH INFRASTRUCTURE AND THE EEC

The Welsh infrastructure was not a balanced regional economic and governmental system but rather consisted almost entirely of Welsh organizations formed within the British bureaucracy or created to deal with it. However, in the 1970s, an opportunity arose to augment the Welsh infrastructure in relation to another bureaucracy, that of the European Economic Community. Before Britain joined the EEC, Plaid Cymru had opposed entry under terms negotiated by an English government but reserved a final decision until Wales could be represented at a conference to discuss terms for Welsh entry (Butt Philip, 1975, pp. 119, 182–183). The party continued to oppose the EEC during the 1975 referendum on a possible British withdrawal. However, immediately following the vote, which favored remaining in the Common Market by a majority of over 60 percent in both England and Wales, the Blaid announced that it would thenceforth concentrate on obtaining representation for Wales in Brussels. Within the month, an office was established in Brussels in conjunction with other nationalist groups representing the Basques, Bretons, and Alsatians and calling itself the Bureau of Unrepresented European Nations (*The Times*, 23 June 1975).

A more important development was the establishment of the Welsh regional office of the EEC, which was officially opened in Cardiff in March 1976. The Cardiff Office of the EEC was made possible by the creation of a program to lessen regional inequality within the European Community. In 1975 the EEC set up the European Regional Development Fund to support new industry and provide grants to improve the infrastructure of disadvantaged regions (European Economic Community, 1976). However, according to the Research Officer for the Cardiff Office of the EEC, "the London EEC Office just was not getting any queries from people in Wales about these funds." Under the urging of the Welsh Office and some Welsh people working in Brussels, the Cardiff Office was set up to inform Welsh industry and local government about the available funds. Furthermore, the office maintained direct contacts with Brussels. "Officially the office in Cardiff is supposed to operate through the one in London, but actually we do not. Gwyn Morgan [the first head of the Cardiff Office] has very good contacts in Brussels, better than the London Office in fact" (interview, 25 April 1977). The relative independence of the Cardiff Office was demonstrated in its blunt criticism of the practice of allowing grants to Welsh authorities to be channelled through the British Treasury, which sometimes enabled the government to cut its own contribution to the Welsh authorities, in direct contradiction of EEC intent[9] (*Western Mail*, 10 June 1977).

The opportunities for Welsh organizations to deal directly with Brussels on Welsh issues were further enhanced by the creation in 1979 of a European Parliament,[10] and such contacts began to be made on a regular basis. Local government representatives made frequent, well-publicized trips to lobby the European bureaucracy and their Euro-MPs. The Welsh Office maintained direct contact with Brussels, and both the Welsh branch of the CBI and the Wales TUC lobbied their parent organizations for the right to represent their special Welsh interests directly within the European bureaucracy and to the Welsh representatives in the European Parliament.

SUMMARY

The growth of the British welfare-state bureaucracy thus made possible the creation of a Welsh administrative infrastructure, and the key organization in this process was the Welsh Office. Its gradual accumulation of powers stimulated, directly or indirectly, the establishment of many other Welsh organizations, most notably the Wales TUC and the Welsh office of the CBI. The existence of this Welsh infrastructure aided the nationalist cause by clarifying the Welsh dimension of many issues, by providing a focus for protest, by giving administrative recognition to a separate Welsh identity, and by providing an argument for political devolution that was not directly linked to nationalist ideology. The pulling back from commitments to the welfare state, signified by the Conservative victory in the 1979 general election, was reflected in nationalist losses in that same period. Subsequent actions of the Conservative government in attacking welfare-state institutions further reduced nationalist political effectiveness. However, the broader nationalist movement managed to regain some ground in its successful campaign for a Welsh television service. Furthermore, the bulk of the Welsh infrastructure remained in place; nor did Plaid Cymru's losses reduce the party to its pre-1966 status. And some scope for enhancing Welsh autonomy and reducing London's authority became available through interaction with the bureaucracy of the European Economic Community.

NOTES

1. In addition, a Welsh National Insurance Commission was set up in 1911, and this became the nucleus for the Welsh Board of Health that was formed in 1919.

2. The first Welsh Day debate was held in 1944. A Minister for Welsh Affairs was appointed in 1951; the post was held jointly with that of Home Secretary, later with that of Minister of Housing and Local Government.

3. A year earlier, in 1955, S. O. Davies, Labour MP for Merthyr Tydfil, had moved a Private Member's Bill for a Welsh Parliament. The bill was badly defeated, with only six Welsh MPs supporting it.

4. For example, the National Executive of the Electrical Trades Union, in 1954, and the Amalgamated Union of Foundry Workers, in 1961 and 1964 (Osmond, 1977, p. 116).

5. On an important vote to end debate on the Bill in the spring of 1977, the government was defeated by the defection of forty Labour MPs who either voted against the measure or abstained. Five of the forty rebel MPs represented Welsh constituencies. However, twenty-one of the total of thirty-six Welsh MPs voted for the motion. This defeat was serious enough to precipitate a motion of 'no confidence', which the government managed to survive.

6. In November 1977, Plaid Cymru MPs were quoted as saying that the Devolution Bill, while inadequate, was still worth having (*Western Mail*, 16 November 1977, 17 November 1977); but in January 1978 the Plaid Cymru National Council "reasserted their aim of full self-government for Wales, rather than devolution" (*Western Mail*, 16 January 1978).

7. In 1978 the name was changed to the Welsh Water Authority.

8. The reference to exported water was not meant to include those sources of water within Wales that were outside the boundary of the authority. The reference was to the Elan Valley reservoirs, which were within the Welsh Water Authority, but because they were built in the 1930s by Birmingham, were leased to Severn-Trent by the Welsh Authority at a nominal annual rate.

9. Proposals to eliminate such practices were subsequently developed by the EEC regional commission.

10. Wales was given four Euro-MPs, a number that nationalists complained was far too small and left Wales underrepresented in comparison to other small European nations, such as Ireland.

6

Conclusions, Comparisons, and Forecasts

The history of the Welsh nationalist movement has been a complex interaction of specific structural factors with group dynamics. This interaction influenced the decisions of various classes of individuals—as voters, as cultural nationalists, and as political activists—and determined the nature of the movement and its successes and failures.

STRUCTURAL STIMULANTS

The most fundamental structural factor governing the political fortunes of the Welsh nationalist movement in the second half of the twentieth century was the development of the welfare state. The primary importance of this development for Welsh nationalism lay not in its creation of a welfare society but in two specific consequences of its growth: it enabled the establishment of Welsh organizations, both within the British welfare bureaucracy and in sectors that dealt with it, resulting in the steady growth of a Welsh bureaucracy which continued through the 1980s; second, it enabled a degree of economic planning for Wales, which eventually took the form of regional development programs. The relationship between economic planning and enhanced nationalist support was largely dependent on the prior development of the Welsh bureaucracy. This bureaucracy itself resulted from two major stimulants: the Welsh language movement forced the establishment of Welsh organizations in certain sectors, in particular education and mass communications; and pressure for devolution of administrative functions to Welsh bodies grew within the British government, especially after the creation of the Welsh Office.

The Welsh infrastructure in education grew out of the movement for Welsh-medium schools initiated in the late 1940s by a Welsh-speaking middle class who based their campaign on provisions of the 1944 Education Act. This movement succeeded, in the decades following World War II, in establishing Welsh-medium primary and secondary schools in all parts of Wales. By the early 1960s, it was drawing support from non-Welsh-speaking, working-class parents; and as pressure from English immigrants increased beginning in the 1970s, the movement also became relevant for parents in the Welsh-speaking areas. Thus, in addition to setting up Welsh-medium schools, the movement encouraged informal networks of language supporters, both Welsh and non-Welsh speakers, in all parts of Wales.

Of the bureaucratic organizations comprising the Welsh educational infrastructure the most influential was the Welsh Joint Education Committee, established in 1948 under the 1944 Education Act, which had responsibility for syllabi and examinations. This infrastructure was relatively unaffected by fluctuations in political nationalism, and even in the 1980s the language movement continued to flourish. In 1986, for example, it succeeded in forcing the establishment and funding, by the Conservative government, of a Welsh Language Education Development Committee to coordinate developments in Welsh-medium education.

In the area of mass communications, the Welsh language movement gradually succeeded in expanding the Welsh-language programming available on radio and television. The creation in 1977 of a separate Welsh service on BBC Radio was a major step forward for this movement. But its most significant accomplishment, following years of direct-action campaigns by Cymdeithas yr Iaith Gymraeg [the Welsh Language Society], was the establishment in 1982 of the Welsh television service (S4C) on the new United Kingdom fourth channel. In addition to increasing the hours of Welsh-language television available, particularly during prime viewing time, this service stimulated the growth of a flourishing private sector of Welsh independent television production companies.

The Welsh language also had provided one basis for some of the earliest reorganization along Welsh lines within the British bureaucracy: separate Welsh departments had been created in education and agriculture in the opening decades of the twentieth century. However, by the 1950s, when some Welsh Labour Party leaders began calling for the creation of a Welsh secretary of state, the office was primarily advocated as a symbolic recognition of Wales's historic national identity and not for either linguistic or administrative reasons. Nevertheless, once established in 1964, the Welsh Office itself began a struggle to aggrandize power within the British bureaucracy, as a result of which it secured decision-making powers regarding policy implementation in a number of areas as they affected Wales. As its influence grew, the Welsh Office also stimulated the restructuring on a Welsh basis of organizations representing special interests, in particular labor and business, as such organizations came to recognize the value of being able to deal directly with it. It was unquestionably the pivotal organization in promoting increased administrative devolution to Wales, and the array of bodies under its supervision in turn provided a major argument for political devolution as a means of democratizing the functions of the growing Welsh bureaucracy.

The growth of a Welsh bureaucracy was important for the Welsh nationalist movement in several respects. First, it provided, for almost the first time since the sixteenth century, official reinforcement for a separate Welsh identity. Second, the organizations comprising this bureaucracy brought a degree of administrative autonomy to Wales. This infrastructure tended to expand as these organizations stimulated the formation of others both inside the bureaucracy and in sectors that dealt closely with it. And as such organizations themselves evolved, they normally struggled to increase their own areas of responsibility, in the process bringing more decision-making powers from the central British bureaucracy into Wales. The shift in the locus of decision making quite often brought the Welsh dimension of particular issues into greater prominence, as well as providing a more readily assailable target for nationalist pressure groups. Finally, the devolution of administrative powers made proposals for a degree of political autonomy appear more realistic, as the next logical step required to democratize the existing bureaucracy.

Though crucial to the development of the nationalist movement in the second half of the twentieth century, the growth of the Welsh bureaucracy was not directly linked to the two periods of internal transformation of Welsh political nationalism or to its accompanying electoral successes. These two periods of nationalist advances, the late 1940s and the decade following the 1966 by-election in Carmarthen, were more closely associated with a second major consequence of the growth of the welfare state—the introduction of extensive economic planning by the central government and, later, the creation of regional development programs. In these two periods, the political nationalist movement attracted new, politically motivated activists and altered its tone and tactics, particularly as projected in its campaign style. These changes were associated with improved electoral performance, which, in the later period, brought some significant nationalist victories.

The economic reorganization undertaken by the central government in the immediate postwar years offered many opportunities to establish Welsh economic units, in certain basic industries as well as public utilities. However, nationalist pressure for Wales to be treated as a unit proved largely ineffective, and what had been a surge in the political nationalist movement ebbed rapidly. In the 1950s, Plaid Cymru's active membership declined as the party returned to its pre-World War II emphasis on cultural preservation.

The party's fortunes were to improve, however, as Welsh unity came to be reflected in government policy as a consequence of the economic programs of the 1960s, which were directed toward increasing employment opportunities in depressed British regions. Given its history of internal colonialism, virtually all of Wales qualified as a development area, thus according it a degree of unity under these new regional development programs. Furthermore, the Welsh infrastructure that had been created in the intervening years, particularly the Welsh Office, greatly strengthened the argument favoring economic planning for Wales as a whole. Instead of reflecting nationalist agitation, however, it represented the position of the Welsh Office, which was seeking control over economic planning for Wales. Thus Plaid Cymru did not have to make a case for Welsh economic planning but could present its own proposals for developing the Welsh economy without appearing unrealistic or utopian. Under such conditions, political nationalism became an attractive choice to relatively large numbers of new activists with political, not cultural, priorities, who in time became the driving force in Plaid Cymru. The Blaid's altered image and message under the prevailing economic climate also increased its appeal to the electorate, resulting in its registering several impressive performances in by-elections in the late 1960s, winning three parliamentary seats by 1974, and enjoying some major successes on district councils.[1]

The political nationalist movement began to show signs of decline again in the late 1970s. By this time, the Labour government, under serious economic pressure, had begun to pull back from government spending commitments, including regional development programs. The elimination, in 1976, of the Regional Employment Premium was a blow to these programs in Wales and elsewhere. The 1979 referendum and general election, which brought some major Plaid Cymru losses in local government as well as a defeat for one of its three MPs, marked the end of this second postwar period of political nationalist resurgence. Successive Conservative governments elected in 1979, in 1983, and in 1987 proved to be deliberate, systematic, and determined in dismantling many of the programs of the welfare state and were particularly opposed to government interference in the economy. Under such circumstances, nationalist political losses were to be expected, in that the possibility of bringing economic decision-making to government bodies in Wales had been the central basis for its enhanced voter appeal.

Cultural nationalism, particularly the Welsh language movement, was less severely affected by these changes. Certainly, the loss of regional development programs and the resulting depletion in the economic base of Welsh-speaking areas had long-term implications for the survival of the language. However, the immediate targets of language activists in the Welsh educational infrastructure were still available, in that government cutbacks were not primarily aimed at dismantling this bureaucracy. Another reason why the language movement suffered less after 1979, as was shown by its success over the establishment of S4C, the Welsh fourth television channel, was that it received broad support from the Welsh middle class, not simply or even primarily from political nationalists, and hence its fortunes were not closely tied to Plaid Cymru.

NATIONALIST GROUPS

Structural factors do not in themselves explain nationalist resurgence and decline; it is rather in their interaction with various collectivities that they produce or influence activists, both political and cultural, and affect the decisions of voters. Although the Welsh Nationalist Party was a small and quite homogeneous body in its early years, neither it nor the broader nationalist movement remained so as they evolved through the years. Both came to contain a number of distinctive groupings, who responded to structural changes in different ways.

The Nationalist Party was initially composed of enthusiasts for Welsh culture and language. They were primarily academics, school teachers and university lecturers, ministers of religion, writers, and others whose professional lives were bound up with the Welsh language, literature, and cultural heritage. Their ideological basis for a separate Welsh state owed much to an informal grouping of Welsh historians who had, beginning about 1911, created a national history for Wales. These historians were not necessarily nationalists themselves but were part of a new academic discipline of Welsh historical studies, made possible by the establishment of several Welsh colleges, which combined to form the University of Wales at the end of the nineteenth century. The Welsh Nationalist Party made extensive use over many decades of the Welsh national history they created both for justification of nationalist goals and for campaign rhetoric. The party itself consisted of a very few members linked by a dense network of social ties. While its avowed purpose was to secure self-government for Wales by working through the electoral system, its principal activity was the maintenance of these social ties and the celebration and enhancement of Welsh culture through events like its annual summer school.

This small organization of cultural nationalists with a political agenda but little genuine political commitment was affected in two periods, the mid-1940s and the late 1960s, by an infusion of nontraditionalists into its membership. Both times the party's image was altered: it became more political, and its message and tactics changed. Whereas the first infusion essentially failed to bring lasting change to the party, the second period transformed it into a genuine political organization as the new members became the mainstream and cultural nationalists themselves became politicized. A major cause of the entry of these new groups into the political nationalist movement, as already discussed, lay in the area of structural changes in the British state, particularly in its involvement in economic development. The first infusion consisted primarily of ex-servicemen returning to Wales after years away during the war. They brought with them a heightened sense of Welsh identity which made them more likely to notice the nationalist party and its message. And they faced relatively open futures in terms of careers and thus could envision improved prospects given the development of Welsh economic structures. The new image and emphasis they helped to introduce into Plaid Cymru's electoral message produced some improvement at the polls. However, the majority of voters foresaw no personal gains in supporting the nationalist program, especially given their commitment and obligations to British-wide unions and the Labour Party. As economic organization in Wales became set along British lines by about 1950, most of these new nationalists, not influenced by social and cultural inducements to remain in the party, became inactive, and Plaid Cymru largely resumed its prewar image.

The second infusion of nontraditionalists into the party, in the late 1960s, had a fundamental and lasting effect on the party, its image, tactics, and activities. The majority of these new members were products of the educational opportunities created by the welfare state for young working-class people, and many were from a socialist background. With heightened expectations and ambitions based on their greater educational achievements, they blamed the limited opportunities within Wales on the prevailing political order and more particularly on the Labour Party. They saw Plaid Cymru and the nationalist message as the way of creating economic opportunity within their own communities. Furthermore, the economic betterment attributable to the new regional development programs made extended, coherent economic planning for Wales appear both more realistic and attractive. This message thus generated broader electoral support, due to its greater realism and improved chance of realization, based on moving toward economic autonomy by degrees instead of having to achieve political independence first.

Apart from the political nationalist movement, other nationalist groups developed primarily around the issue of maintenance of the Welsh language. The most important formal organization in this linguistic nationalism was Cymdeithas yr Iaith Gymraeg. While inspired by Saunders Lewis and having some overlap with Plaid Cymru membership, Cymdeithas yr Iaith was an independent organization whose emergence was not attributable to the same structural factors that had influenced its political counterpart. It appeared in the early 1960s, prior to the start of the Blaid's political surge forward, and consisted primarily of university students, many of whom were studying Welsh language, literature, and history. These individuals were able to accept the personal costs involved in the nonviolent, direct-action campaign which was launched to gain official recognition for their language. While their campaigns were a response to the intrusive nature of the welfare state and its tendency to standardize on an English mold, language activists were not primarily stimulated by its economic programs, as Plaid Cymru had been. Nevertheless, they benefitted the political nationalist movement in several ways. They won recognition for the most salient and arguably the most important carrier of Welsh identity; they revealed one form of institutionalized oppression claimed to be inherent in British rule; and they provided an outlet for nationalists discouraged by lack of progress in the political arena. Cymdeithas yr Iaith was hampered somewhat by the relatively brief period in which most of its members were active before assuming family and career obligations. Its history also reflected, to a degree, the decline in student activism in Western societies in the 1970s and 1980s. However, linguistic issues continued to be highly salient in Wales; the movement's principal targets in the Welsh bureaucracy were not eliminated by government economies; and Cymdeithas yr Iaith, as a pressure group, was not overly dependent on broad public support. Thus, this organization did not experience the same fluctuations in strength and effectiveness as did the political nationalist movement.

The other major linguistic nationalist grouping, that seeking to establish Welsh-medium education, was very different in character. It consisted not of a single organization, but rather of many different organizations, each set up to pursue relatively limited goals, such as establishing a particular Welsh-medium school. It was more broadly based, in terms of age, class, and locality, and it primarily relied on traditional pressure-group tactics, rather than direct action, to secure its aims. This movement was initially led by a Welsh-speaking middle class, living in anglicized areas, who wanted to ensure that their children received their education in Welsh. Their leadership, combined with the high quality of the Welsh-medium schools they established and the perception that an ability to speak Welsh brought increased employment opportunities, particularly in relatively prestigious sectors such as communications, enabled the movement to expand well beyond its initial boundaries of class and geographic area. The strength of the Welsh schools movement was not directly related to political nationalism. It contributed to the overall nationalist movement by bolstering and expanding the use of the Welsh language among young people, as well as being primarily responsible for the growth of a Welsh educational infrastructure. However, its successes in no way translated directly into support for Plaid Cymru. In fact, perhaps one of its greatest contributions to Welsh nationalism was its ability to win support for a central nationalist aim, that of language maintenance, even among those who were totally opposed to nationalist political goals.

SOME COMPARISONS

An intrusive bureaucracy, such as that associated with the development of the welfare state, has been linked to the growth of ethnic political movements worldwide, even among groups lacking a territorial base. The American state fostered ethnic solidarity by creating ethnic categories for the census, in particular Hispanics and Native Americans, and provided foci for ethnic protest by establishing organizations such as the Bureau of Indian Affairs (Enloe, 1981). The appearance, comparatively early in the twentieth century, of nationalist movements in the colonial territories of European states was a consequence of the highly intrusive nature of colonial bureaucracies and of their early adoption of many of the principles and administrative techniques, including economic planning, later implemented domestically (Fieldhouse, 1966, pp. 376–379; A. D. Smith, 1976, p. 14). The success of the anti-colonial nationalist movements did not result in any fundamental change in the colonial administrative apparatus but rather transferred control over it to a native nationalist elite. And since the boundaries of most of these new Third World states had originally been set by their colonizers and normally contained many different ethnic groups, the post-independence period saw the emergence of a large number of schismatic ethnic nationalist movements (cf. Olorunsola, 1972).

The ethnic political movements that have arisen among the historic nationalities of Western Europe differed from those of the colonial territories in that bureaucratic organization developed specifically for these regions was achieved as a result of nationalist pressure rather than being initially established by the central state for purely administrative purposes. The rationale for establishing Welsh organizations within the British bureaucracy, especially in the early stages, relied heavily on the need for special accommodations for Wales due to the existence of the Welsh language. And the Welsh language continued to provide the basis for an extensive Welsh infrastructure within education as well as in the communications industry. In general, education was one of the first sectors into which central states began to extend their influence in the late nineteenth and early twentieth centuries, and thus a separate language was a particularly useful attribute for an ethnic group. The Welsh experience suggests that if an ethnic language becomes the language of instruction, rather than being confined to being taught as a separate subject, the consequent requirements for separate syllabi, materials, and examinations can be used to achieve significant restructuring along ethnic lines of the educational system. In contrast, the national history of an ethnic group is not as likely to prove a useful resource in this regard in that it can too readily be accommodated within the state educational system by appending it to existing history courses.

The lack of such an effective cultural resource as a viable separate language accounts for the weakness of Cornish nationalism, both cultural and political. Local legend at least has it that the last speaker of Cornish as a mother tongue died in the eighteenth century, and nationalist attempts in the second half of the twentieth century to revive the language, limited by the absence of a pool of native speakers, were not successful in gaining significant state bureaucratic recognition for Cornwall or in bolstering the nationalist movement. The nature of other regional cultural distinctions may also limit their potential to provide a foundation for some form of ethnic political movement. Separate regional cultures, based on attributes like regional accent, distinctive food preferences, and distinctive personal lifestyles, even when combined with a history of economic exploitation, such as existed in the north of England, have not been sufficient to support political separatist movements. Such cultural materials cannot readily be linked to the public realm, as was the Welsh language, to win state bureaucratic reinforcement of the region's distinctiveness. Nor do they have much appeal, or much utility in career terms, for the ethnic intellectual leadership, who generally must lay the theoretical foundation for a popular movement to develop.

Thus the distinctive cultures of historic nationalities make a substantive contribution to the development of political nationalist movements, primarily by helping to win a degree of official recognition, in the form of bureaucratic organizations based on the ethnic territory. However, not all ethnic nationalist movements have had to rely on distinctive cultural attributes to provide them with such an ethnic infrastructure, and in these cases the role of culture in both ideology and electoral tactics is much reduced. Regions that were incorporated relatively late in the process of state formation often retained a significant amount of indigenous organization. Scotland, for example, became part of Great Britain by treaty in 1707 and managed to keep its own banking, educational, and legal systems. An alternative basis for an ethnic infrastructure is provided by states with a federal form of government, in contrast to that which is possible under such highly centralized governments as Britain and France. If the ethnic region coincides with provincial boundaries, an ethnic nationalist movement will likely attempt to gain control of the provincial government, which constitutes a ready-made set of organizations based on the ethnic region. The ethnic nationalist movements that gained prominence in Quebec and among the Francophones in New Brunswick in the 1970s were both affected by Canada's federal form of government. Whereas the Quebecois achieved a high degree of autonomy by gaining control over the existing Quebec provincial government, the Acadian movement in New Brunswick was largely confined to winning greater recognition for Francophones on the basis of distinctive cultural criteria, mainly the French language, within a provincial government that, because of the high proportion of Anglophones in its population, could not in itself provide an organizational base for the movement (cf. Cimino, 1978).

Nationalist movements that have in situ an indigenous organizational structure on which to base themselves are generally in a better position to surge forward electorally when other structural factors favor such growth. The second major structural stimulant stemming from the development of the welfare state was the prospect of economic planning for the ethnic region and the chance to achieve ethnic economic organization. The gains made by the Scottish Nationalist Party in the 1974 general election, for example, when it jumped from three to eleven MPs, were far in excess of those made by Plaid Cymru. However, its losses, when such economic prospects vanished, were also predictably greater; the SNP dropped to two MPs, the same number as Plaid Cymru, in 1979. Furthermore, those nationalist movements that do not have preservation of a threatened language or culture as a major aspect of their program lack an alternative outlet for nationalist campaigning during periods of political nationalist decline.

A final factor leading to differences among ethnic nationalist movements is the nature of the economic history of the ethnic region. Those regions that underwent an internal colonial form of exploitation were seldom able to develop any significant native capitalist base, even after the major markers of internal colonialism had been removed, or greatly attenuated, through state action. And nationalist movements in such regions tended to develop a more socialist position than those whose form of incorporation by the central state had allowed for the growth of a native capitalist class. Scotland, in contrast to Wales, had a relatively prosperous capitalist class in the nineteenth century (Nairn, 1977, pp. 149, 199–207); and the twentieth-century Scottish Nationalist Party emerged as a far less left-leaning movement, in overall tone and policies, than did Plaid Cymru.

Although there were some socialists among Scottish nationalists, their influence was far weaker than that of socialists in the Blaid. In 1982, for example, when Plaid Cymru was affirming its commitment to establishing a decentralized socialist state in Wales as one of its basic aims, the SNP Conference expelled a socialist ginger group (the '79' group) from its ranks.

THE FUTURE

Since the Welsh nationalist movement consists of a variety of groups responding to different structural factors, the future of Welsh nationalism will in reality be a plurality of futures. The language movement will doubtless continue to be the most dynamic arena of nationalist activity for some time, with campaigns such as that for a new Welsh Language Act in the forefront. The battle to maintain the vitality of the Welsh language in its 'heartland' will probably be won or lost by the end of the twentieth century. With the aim of ensuring a continued supply of affordable homes for local people and limiting the vastly increased flow of relatively affluent immigrants from England, language activists have come to recognize the need for the adoption of planning regulations that will respect indigenous cultural and economic circumstances. There have been some indications that local authorites and Welsh Office planning inspectors are sympathetic to these demands. In the meantime, language supporters have also turned their attention toward the possibility of absorbing these immigrants into a more cosmopolitan, but still Welsh, cultural milieu (e.g., Dafis, 1985; G. Evans, 1988a). Some achievements in this direction would greatly enhance the prospects for maintaining the integrity of the Welsh-speaking heartland.

The growth of the Welsh-medium schools, particularly in the valleys of southeast Wales, has been one of the major successes of the Welsh language movement. These valleys are virtually untouched by the recent influx of English immigrants that is such a major problem for the rest of Wales; and their population, while predominantly English speaking, is overwhelmingly Welsh in its self-identity. These areas could become an important source of strength for the language movement if activists can find ways of overcoming two major stumbling blocks. The young Welsh speakers coming out of Welsh-medium schools often have difficulty finding employment in their home communities and have to move elsewhere. Of those who do remain, there are few opportunities to speak Welsh either socially or in work. Some funds to improve the employment situation and to encourage the Welsh language in the region have been forthcoming from the European Economic Community's program for the regions. While the effectiveness of such programs has yet to be assessed, they appear to offer some prospects for helping to strengthen the position of the Welsh language in a part of Wales outside the traditional linguistic heartland.

Another likely sector for growth in the broader Welsh nationalist movement is that of the Welsh bureaucracy. While cuts in government spending adversely affect many aspects of Welsh life, such as social services and employment, they do not threaten the existence of the Welsh bureaucracy. The Welsh Office and other Welsh organizations within the bureaucracy will continue to flourish, affirming Welsh identity by their very existence and bringing Wales a degree of administrative autonomy by their self-aggrandizement of power and influence. Furthermore, they continue to provide both a reason for an elected Welsh assembly, as a means of democratizing the Welsh bureaucracy, and a structure that helps to make such proposals appear more evolutionary than revolutionary. Yet another movement for such an assembly, which appeared in the late 1980s, may have a better chance of success than the assembly proposals developed by the Labour Party in the late 1970s in that it is spearheaded by the Wales TUC and is attempting to involve local government and a spectrum of other organizations.

Such an assembly, assuming it had some economic powers, probably offers the best hope for a revival of popular appeal for Welsh political nationalism in the near future. Linked as Plaid Cymru's electoral success appears to be with prospects for gaining a degree of control over Welsh economic affairs, the party's chances for increasing its support at the polls under the current British government and British economic climate are slim indeed. Nevertheless, the electoral gains made in the early 1970s appear secure, especially given the addition of a third parliamentary constituency to the nationalist fold provided by the victory of Ieuan Wyn Jones in Ynys Môn in the 1987 general election. And the comparative maturity of the Blaid as a political party, gained in the 1960s and 1970s, will allow it to continue to influence Welsh politics, by acting essentially as a pressure group.

However, Plaid Cymru is unlikely to make any significant electoral advances without itself creating, or having provided by external factors, some basis for establishing Welsh economic unity and control over economic decision making. Some nationalists have suggested developing a cooperative economy, modelled on the successful Basque venture of the 1920s and 1930s, as an alternative to existing economic structures (e.g., Ifan, 1988; Orwig, 1987). Such a community-based plan would fit well with the Blaid's advocacy of what they have designated decentralized socialism. But any successful implementation would have to overcome some major difficulties in a too close adherence to the Basque model: first, the Basque region was relatively prosperous in comparison to most of the rest of Spain, unlike the position of Wales within Britain; and, second, the conditions of the world economy, particularly as regards the mobility of international capital, are quite different in the late twentieth century from those obtaining in the 1930s.

One other potential source of strength for political nationalism in Wales may lie in its relation to the European Economic Community and the European Parliament. To the degree that the Welsh economy comes to be more directly influenced by its position in the European economy than by its position in Britain, and to the degree that the EEC increases its economic assistance directly to the regions, nationalist claims about the underrepresentation of Wales in Europe—resulting from its status as a mere region of Britain rather than being an independent nation like Ireland—may make an impact on the electorate and offer a new pathway forward for Welsh political nationalism.

NOTE

1. In 1976, Plaid Cymru won control of the Merthyr Tydfil district council and became the party of government on the Rhymney district council, both in Mid Glamorgan, in the southeast. It also became the party of government on three district councils in Gwynedd, in northwest Wales.

Appendixes

Appendix A
Plaid Cymru Electoral History:
General Elections 1945–1987

Election	Percent of Total Vote	Number of Candidates	Average Percent of Vote in Constituencies Contested
1945	1.1	7	9.1
1950	1.2	7	6.8
1951	0.7	4	6.1
1955	3.1	11	11.3
1959	5.2	20	10.3
1964	4.8	23	8.4
1966	4.3	20	8.7
1970	11.5	36	12.4
Feb 1974	10.7	36	11.7
Oct 1974	10.8	36	11.6
1979	8.1	36	10.1
1983	7.8	38	8.2
1987	7.3	38	7.9

Sources: Craig (1969, 1976); Dod's Parliamentary Companion (1950–1988).

Appendix B
Plaid Cymru Performance in
By-elections in Welsh Constitutencies 1945–1987

Year	Constituency	Percent	Second?
1945	Caernarfon Boroughs	24.8	yes
1945	Neath	16.2	yes
1946	Ogmore	29.4	yes
1946	Aberdare	20.0	yes
1955	Wrexham	11.3	no
1956	Newport	3.8	no
1957	Carmarthen	11.5	no
1958	Pontypool	10.2	no
1962	Montgomery	6.2	no
1963	Swansea East	5.2	no
1965	Abertillery	6.7	no
1966	Carmarthen	39.0	*
1967	Rhondda West	39.9	yes
1968	Caerphilly	40.4	yes
1972	Merthyr Tydfil	37.1	yes
1982	Gower	8.7	no
1984	Cynon Valley	10.9	no
1985	Brecon and Radnor	1.1	no

*Plaid Cymru victory

Sources: Craig (1969); Dod's Parliamentary Companion (1950–1988).

Appendix C
Plaid Cymru Percent of Total Vote by Constituency:
General Elections 1945–1987

Constituency	1945[a]	1950	1951	1955	1959	1964
Aberavon					6.6	4.6
Aberdare		7.5	6.1	9.4	8.3	7.2
Abertillery				4.1		
Anglesey				7.5	14.6	6.4
Barry						
Bedwellty						
Brecon and Radnor						5.2
Caernarfon	5.4	13.1		16.5	21.2	21.4
Caerphilly					8.9	11.0
Cardiff North					5.1	2.1
Cardiff Northwest[b]						
Cardiff Southeast						
Cardiff West						
Cardigan					12.8	10.9
Carmarthen				7.8	5.2	11.6
Conway				7.8	7.6	8.3
Denbigh					7.2	7.9
Ebbw Vale						
Flint East						
Flint West					4.0	3.0
Gower				10.6	9.1	6.5
Llanelli		3.8	6.9	12.5	13.8	7.0
Meirioneth	10.3	11.1		22.1	23.0	16.8
Merthyr Tydfil						9.3
Monmouth						
Montgomery						8.5
Neath	7.3					
Newport						
Ogmore	5.6					5.3
Pembroke					4.3	3.4
Pontypool					6.6	
Pontypridd						
Rhondda East[c]	6.1	3.9			8.8	8.2
Rhondda West		6.6	7.7	15.3	17.0	10.2
Swansea East					10.5	8.4
Swansea West						
Wrexham		1.7	3.6	10.4	12.2	8.9

Appendix C
(continued)

Constituency	1966	1970	Feb 1974	Oct 1974	1979
Aberavon		8.4	12.2	8.5	3.8
Aberdare	8.6	30.0	29.9	21.3	9.8
Abertillery		6.2	10.9	9.0	7.9
Anglesey	9.6	22.1	21.7	19.1	20.3
Barry		7.1	3.4	3.3	2.1
Bedwellty		10.0	7.7	8.0	6.6
Brecon and Radnor	6.0	5.4	4.7	5.2	2.2
Caernarfon	21.7	33.4	40.5[d]	42.6[d]	49.7[d]
Caerphilly	11.1	28.5	27.5	24.5	14.9
Cardiff North		4.1	4.6	4.6	3.0
Cardiff Northwest[b]			3.4	3.7	2.1
Cardiff Southeast		5.1	3.0	2.4	1.6
Cardiff West		10.1	5.5	5.5	10.4
Cardigan	8.1	19.6	13.3	13.2	14.5
Carmarthen	16.1	30.1	34.3	45.1[d]	32.0
Conway	6.7	10.8	10.1	11.8	8.6
Denbigh	6.1	11.0	8.1	11.9	9.3
Ebbw Vale		5.9	5.9	7.3	6.5
Flint East	1.9	4.4	1.9	3.2	1.9
Flint West	3.7	6.9	4.4	4.8	3.2
Gower		14.0	8.3	10.0	7.2
Llanelli	10.9	16.7	12.0	13.7	7.4
Meirioneth	11.4	24.3	34.6[d]	42.5[d]	40.8[d]
Merthyr Tydfil	11.5	9.5	22.9	14.8	9.4
Monmouth		2.5	1.5	1.4	1.0
Montgomery	7.4	11.8	8.3	9.3	8.5
Neath		10.1	21.5	17.9	15.3
Newport		3.7	1.5	2.1	0.8
Ogmore		11.7	9.6	8.4	4.4
Pembroke	5.0	6.7	4.8	4.5	2.5
Pontypool		5.3	3.1	5.6	2.6
Pontypridd		10.4	8.5	7.6	3.8
Rhondda East[c]	7.5	24.3			
Rhondda West	8.7	14.0	12.9	7.7	8.4
Swansea East	6.8	10.2	11.9	9.5	6.0
Swansea West		6.2	3.6	3.6	1.9
Wrexham	4.5	5.3	4.5	5.1	2.8

Appendix C
(continued)

Constituency	1983[a]	1987
Aberavon	4.6	2.8
Alyn and Deeside	0.9	1.0
Blaenau Gwent	3.8	3.7
Brecon and Radnor	1.7	1.3
Bridgend	3.2	2.3
Caernarfon	52.7[d]	57.1[d]
Caerphilly	13.6	8.1
Cardiff Central	1.8	1.3
Cardiff North	2.4	1.6
Cardiff South & Penarth	1.6	1.3
Cardiff West	2.1	1.6
Carmarthen	27.1	23.0
Ceredigion & Pembroke North	12.9	16.2
Clwyd Northwest	3.7	4.0
Clwyd Southwest	8.6	8.5
Conwy	10.4	7.8
Cynon Valley	9.3	6.7
Delyn	3.2	2.5
Gower	3.2	2.8
Islwyn	4.0	4.8
Llanelli	12.2	10.2
Meirionydd Nant Conwy	39.2[d]	40.0[d]
Merthyr Tydfil and Rhymney	4.8	4.7
Monmouth	1.1	0.8
Montgomery	5.3	4.5
Neath	7.2	6.4
Newport East	1.7	1.1
Newport West	1.1	0.8
Ogmore	7.9	4.4
Pembroke	2.0	2.0
Pontypridd	4.7	5.3
Rhondda	10.2	8.9
Swansea East	3.7	2.7
Swansea West	1.9	2.0
Torfaen	2.1	1.3
Vale of Glamorgan	2.3	1.8
Wrexham	2.6	1.1
Ynys Mon	33.3	43.2[d]

[a]There were major boundary changes after 1945 and 1983.
[b]Created in 1974.
[c]Rhondda East and Rhondda West were consolidated in 1974.
[d]Plaid Cymru victory.

Sources: Craig (1969); Dod's Parliamentary Companion (1950–1987).

References

Adam, H. (1984). Rational choice in ethnic mobilization: A critique. *International Migration Review, 18*(2), 377–381.

Ashby, A. W., & Evans, I. L. (1944). *The agriculture of Wales and Monmouthshire*. Cardiff, Wales: University of Wales Press.

Aull, C. H. (1979). Ethnic nationalism in Wales: An analysis of the factors governing the politicization of ethnic identity (Doctoral dissertation, Duke University, 1978). *Dissertation Abstracts International, 39*(9), 5591A.

Balandier, G. (1966). The colonial situation: A theoretical approach. In I. Wallerstein (Ed.), *Social change: The colonial situation* (pp. 34–61). New York: John Wiley.

Balsom, D., & Madgwick, P. J. (1978). Wales, European integration and devolution. In M. Kolinsky (Ed.), *Divided loyalties—British regional assertion and European integration* (pp. 70–89). Manchester, England: Manchester University Press.

Barrow, G. W. S. (1956). *Feudal Britain: The completion of the medieval kingdoms 1066–1314*. London: Edward Arnold.

Betts, C. (1976). *Culture in crisis: The future of the Welsh language*. Upton, Wirral, Merseyside, England: The Ffynnon Press.

Bowen, E. G. (1959). The age of the saints. In A. J. Roderick (Ed.), *Wales through the ages, volume 1* (pp. 60–66). Llandybie, Carmarthenshire, Wales: Christopher Davies.

Bowen, E. G., & Carter, H. (1975). The distribution of the Welsh language in 1971: An analysis. *Geography, 60*(1), 1–15.

Broady, M. (1977). *'Welsh water': The politics of water supply*. Paper presented at the meeting of the Regional Studies Association Conference on Water Planning and the Regions, London, England (March).

Bruce, M. (1968). *The coming of the welfare state* (4th ed.). London: B. T. Batsford.
Bulpitt, J. (1983). *Territory and power in the United Kingdom: An interpretation.* Manchester, England: Manchester University Press.
Butt Philip, A. (1975). *The Welsh question: Nationalism in Welsh politics, 1945–1970.* Cardiff, Wales: University of Wales Press.
Carter, H. (1966). *The towns of Wales.* Cardiff, Wales: University of Wales Press.
Chadwick, N. K. (1959). The Welsh dynasties in the dark ages. In A. J. Roderick (Ed.), *Wales through the ages, volume 1* (pp. 50–59). Llandybie, Carmarthenshire, Wales: Christopher Davies.
Cimino, L. F. (1978). Ethnic nationalism among the Acadians of New Brunswick: An analysis of ethnic political development (Doctoral dissertation, Duke University, 1977). *Dissertation Abstracts International, 39*(3), 1685A–1686A.
Clark, R. P. (1980). Euzkadi: Basque nationalism in Spain since the Civil War. In C. R. Foster (Ed.), *Nations without a state: Ethnic minorities in western Europe* (pp. 75–100). New York: Praeger.
Conkling, E. C. (1964). The measurement of diversification. In G. Manners (Ed.), *South Wales in the sixties: Studies in industrial geography* (pp. 161–183). New York: Macmillan.
Connor, W. (1984). *The national question in Marxist–Leninist theory and strategy.* Princeton, NJ: Princeton University Press.
Craig, F. W. S. (1969). *British parliamentary election results 1918–1949.* Glasgow, Scotland: Political Reference Publications.
Craig, F. W. S. (1976). *British electoral facts 1885–1975.* London: Macmillan.
Cymdeithas yr Iaith Gymraeg (1974). *Bywyd i'r iaith: Welsh must live.* Caerphilly, Wales.
Dafis, C. (1985). Lessons for the language, 2: Aliens in our own land. *Radical Wales* (Winter), 14–15.
Das Gupta, J. (1970). *Language conflict and national development: Group politics and national language policy in India.* Bombay: Oxford University Press.
Davies, C. (1973). Cymdeithas yr Iaith Gymraeg. In M. Stephens (Ed.), *The Welsh language today* (pp. 248–263). Llandysul, Wales: Gomer.
Davies, D. H. (1983). *The Welsh Nationalist Party 1925–1945: A call to nationhood.* Cardiff, Wales: University of Wales Press.
Davies, D. J. (1949). *Towards an economic democracy.* Cardiff, Wales: Plaid Cymru.
Davies, D. J. (1958). An economic policy for Wales. In C. Thomas (Ed.), *Towards Welsh freedom: Twenty-seven articles by Dr. D. J. Davies* (pp. 57–65). Cardiff, Wales: Plaid Cymru. (Original work published 1931.)
Davies, D. J., & Davies, N. (1947). *Can Wales afford self government?* (rev. ed.). Cardiff, Wales: Plaid Cymru. (Original work published 1939.)
Davies, D. J., & Richards, H. P. (1948). *The Welsh coal industry: Memorandum submitted to the executive committee of the Welsh Nationalist Party.* Cardiff, Wales: Welsh Nationalist Party.

Davies, G. (1973). *The story of the Urdd (The Welsh League of Youth) 1922–1972*. Aberystwyth, Wales: Cwmni Urdd Gobaith Cymru.

Davies, G., & Thomas, I. (1976). *Overseas investment in Wales: The welcome invasion*. Swansea, Wales: Christopher Davies.

Davies, I. (1944). *A trade union for Wales*. Caernarfon, Wales: Plaid Genedlaethol Cymru.

Deutsch, K. W. (1942). The trend of European nationalism—the language aspect. *American Political Science Review, 36*, 533–541.

Dickie-Clark, H. F. (1984). The debate over the theory of rational choice. *International Migration Review, 18*(1), 164–170.

Dodd, A. H. (1971). *The industrial revolution in north Wales* (3rd ed.). Cardiff, Wales: University of Wales Press.

Dod's Parliamentary Companion (1950–1988). *Dod's parliamentary companion*. Hurst Green, East Sussex, England.

Douglass, W. A., & Da Silva, M. (1971). Basque nationalism. In O. Pi-Sunyer (Ed.), *The limits of integration: Ethnicity and nationalism in modern Europe* (pp. 147–186). Amherst, MA: Department of Anthropology, University of Massachusetts.

Driscoll, J. (1962). Steel. In B. Thomas (Ed.), *The Welsh economy: Studies in expansion* (pp. 114–137). Cardiff, Wales: University of Wales Press.

Duncan, G. (1982). The Marxist theory of the state. In G. H. R. Parkinson (Ed.), *Marx and marxisms* (pp. 129–143). Cambridge, England: Cambridge University Press.

Dunleavy, P. (1981). Alternative theories of liberal democratic politics: The pluralist–marxist debate in the 1980s. In D. Potter (Ed.), *Society and the social sciences* (pp. 200–220). London: Routledge & Kegan Paul.

Edwards, H. T. (1976). *Yr Eisteddfod: Cyfrol ddathlu wythganmlwyddiant yr Eisteddfod, 1176–1976* [The Eisteddfod: Commemorative volume for the eight-hundredth anniversary, 1176–1976]. Cardiff, Wales: Llys yr Eisteddfod Genedlaethol.

Elton, G. R. (1955). *England under the Tudors*. London: Methuen.

England, J. W. (1972). The inheritance. In G. Humphrys, *South Wales* (pp. 11–35). Newton Abbott, England: David & Charles.

Enloe, C. (1981). The growth of the state and ethnic mobilization: The American experience. *Ethnic and Racial Studies, 4*(2), 123–136.

European Economic Community (1976). *Wales in Europe*. Cardiff, Wales: Commission of the European Communities.

Evans, G. (1956). *Save Cwm Tryweryn for Wales*. Cardiff, Wales: Plaid Cymru.

Evans, G. (1974). *Land of my fathers: 2000 years of Welsh history* (E. Garlick & R. Garlick, trans.). Swansea, Wales: John Penry. (Original work published 1971.)

Evans, G. (1988a). Argyfwng y mewnfudo [The immigration crisis]. *Y Faner* (June 24), 7–8.

Evans, G. (1988b). The 1536 Act of Incorporation and the Welsh language. *Planet: The Welsh Internationalist, 68*, 54–58.

Fenn, R. W. D. (1976). The age of the saints. In D. Walker (Ed.), *A history of the Church in Wales* (pp. 1–23). Penarth, South Glamorgan, Wales: Church in

Wales Publications, Education and Communications Centre.
Fieldhouse, D. K. (1966). *The colonial empires from the eighteenth century*. New York: Dell.
Fisher, H. A. L. (1936). *A history of Europe*. London: Edward Arnold.
Fishman, J. A. (1972). *Language and nationalism: Two integrative essays*. Rowley, MA: Newbury House.
Fishman, J. A., Gertner, M. H., Lowy, E. G., & Milan, W. G. (1985). *The rise and fall of the ethnic revival: Perspectives on language and ethnicity*. Berlin: Mouton.
Foster, C. R. (1980). *Nations without a state: Ethnic minorities in western Europe*. New York: Praeger.
Foster, I. L. (1959). The Welsh awakening. In A. J. Roderick (Ed.), *Wales through the ages, volume 1* (pp. 88–96). Llandybie, Carmarthenshire, Wales: Christopher Davies.
Fox, R. G., Aull, C., & Cimino, L. (1980). Ethnic nationalism and the welfare state. In C. F. Keyes (Ed.), *Ethnic change* (pp. 198–245). Seattle, WA: University of Washington Press.
Fraser, D. (1973). *The evolution of the British welfare state: A history of social policy since the industrial revolution*. London: Macmillan.
Friedlander, D. (1970). The spread of urbanization in England and Wales, 1851–1951. *Population studies, 24*(3), 423–443.
Gans, H. J. (1962). *Urban villagers*. New York: Free Press of Glencoe.
Glazer, N., & Moynihan, D. P. (1975). Introduction. In N. Glazer & D. P. Moynihan (Eds.), *Ethnicity: Theory and experience* (pp. 1–26). Cambridge, MA: Harvard University Press.
Gordon, M. M. (1975). Toward a general theory of racial and ethnic group relations. In N. Glazer & D. P. Moynihan (Eds.), *Ethnicity: Theory and experience* (pp. 84–110). Cambridge, MA: Harvard University Press.
Great Britain (1967). *Primary education in Wales: A report of the Central Advisory Council for Education (Wales)*. London: Her Majesty's Stationery Office.
Great Britain (1972). *Bilingual traffic signs: Report of the Committee of Inquiry under the chairmanship of Roderic Bowen, Esq., Q.C., M.A. Ll.D. 1971–72*. Cardiff, Wales: Her Majesty's Stationery Office.
Great Britain (1975a). *Digest of Welsh statistics*. London: Her Majesty's Stationery Office.
Great Britain (1975b). *Welsh Development Agency Act*. London: Her Majesty's Stationery Office.
Great Britain (1976). *Self-government for Wales, speech by Mr. Gwynfor Evans, MP, House of Commons, Monday 13th December 1976, extract from the official report*. London: Her Majesty's Stationery Office.
Green, L. (1982). Rational nationalists. *Political Studies, 30*(2), 236–246.
Grigg, J. (1973). *The young Lloyd George*. Berkeley: University of California Press.
Hardin, R. (1982). *Collective action*. Baltimore: Johns Hopkins University Press.
Hardinge, L. (1972). *The Celtic Church in Britain*. London: S.P.C.K., for the Church Historical Society.

Hechter, M. (1975). *Internal colonialism: The Celtic fringe in British national development, 1536–1966*. Berkeley: University of California Press.
Hechter, M. (1983). A theory of group solidarity. In M. Hechter (Ed.), *The microfoundations of macrosociology* (pp. 16–57). Philadelphia: Temple University Press.
Hechter, M. (1985). Internal colonialism revisited. In E. A. Tiryakian & R. Rogowski (Eds.), *New nationalisms of the developed West: Toward explanation* (pp. 17–26). Boston: Allen & Unwin.
Hechter, M., & Friedman, D. (1984a). Does rational choice theory suffice? Response to Adam. *International Migration Review, 18*(2), 381–388.
Hechter, M., & Friedman, D. (1984b). Response to Dickie-Clark. *International Migration Review, 18*(1), 171–173.
Hechter, M., Friedman, D., & Appelbaum, M. (1982). A theory of ethnic collective action. *International Migration Review, 16*(2), 412–434.
Hechter, M., & Levi, M. (1979). The comparative analysis of ethnoregional movements. *Ethnic and Racial Studies, 2*(3), 260–274.
Hobsbawm, E. (1968). *Industry and empire: The making of modern English society, volume 2, 1750 to the present day*. New York: Random House.
Hobsbawm, E. (1983). Mass-producing traditions: Europe, 1870–1914. In E. Hobsbawm & T. Ranger (Eds.), *The invention of tradition* (pp. 263–307). Cambridge, England: Cambridge University Press.
Hodges, T. M. (1969a). Early banking in Cardiff. In W. E. Minchinton (Ed.), *Industrial south Wales, 1750–1914: Essays in Welsh economic history* (pp. 163–172). London: Frank Cass.
Hodges, T. M. (1969b). The history of the Newport and Caerleon Savings Bank, 1839–88. In W. E. Minchinton (Ed.), *Industrial south Wales, 1750–1914: Essays in Welsh economic history* (pp. 190–205). London: Frank Cass.
Houlder, C. (1975). *Wales: An archaeological guide*. Park Ridge, NJ: Noyes Press.
Humphreys, E. (n.d.). *The Welsh condition*. Cardiff, Wales: Plaid Cymru. (Original work published 1970.)
Humphrys, G. (1972). *South Wales*. Newton Abbot, Devon, England: David & Charles.
Ifan, S. (1988). Y raj newydd [The new raj]. *Y Faner* (June 3), 6–7.
Iwan, D. (1981). *Dafydd Iwan*. Caernarfon, Wales: Gwynedd.
Jackson, K. (1959). The dawn of the Welsh language. In A. J. Roderick (Ed.), *Wales through the ages, volume 1* (pp. 34–41). Llandybie, Carmarthenshire, Wales: Christopher Davies.
Jenkins, Dafydd (1975). *Tân yn Llŷn* [Fire in Lleyn]. Cardiff, Wales: Plaid Cymru.
Jenkins, David (1971). *The agricultural community in south-west Wales at the turn of the twentieth century*. Cardiff, Wales: University of Wales Press.
Jenkins, R. T. (1935). The development of nationalism in Wales. *The Sociological Review, 27*(2), 163–182.
Jenkins, R. T., & Ramage, H. M. (1951). *A history of the Honourable Society of Cymmrodorion and of the Gwyneddigion and Cymreigyddion Societies (1751–1951)*. London: The Honourable Society of Cymmrodorion.
Jones, D. G. (1973a). His politics. In A. R. Jones & G. Thomas (Eds.), *Presenting*

Saunders Lewis (pp. 23–78). Cardiff, Wales: University of Wales Press.
Jones, D.G. (1973b). The Welsh language movement. In M. Stephens (Ed.), *The Welsh language today* (pp. 264–318). Llandysul, Wales: Gomer.
Jones, J. E. (1970). *Tros Gymru: J. E. a'r Blaid* [For Wales: J. E. and the Blaid]. Swansea, Wales: John Penry.
Jones, L. (1962). Coal. In B. Thomas (Ed.), *The Welsh economy: Studies in expansion* (pp. 89–113). Cardiff, Wales: University of Wales Press.
Khleif, B. B. (1975). *Ethnic boundaries, identity, and schooling: A socio-cultural study of Welsh–English relations*. Durham, NH: University of New Hampshire.
Levi, M., & Hechter, M. (1985). A rational choice approach to the rise and decline of ethnoregional political parties. In E. A. Tiryakian & R. Rogowski (Eds.), *New nationalisms of the developed West: Toward explanation* (pp. 128–146). Boston: Allen & Unwin.
Lewis, R. (1969). *Second-class citizen: A selection of highly personal opinions mainly concerning the two languages of Wales*. Llandysul, Wales: Gomer.
Lewis, S. (1932). *Braslun o hanes llenyddiaeth Gymraeg hyd 1535* [An outline of the history of Welsh literature to 1535]. Cardiff, Wales: University of Wales Press.
Lewis, S. (1973). The fate of the language (G. A. Williams, trans.). In A. R. Jones & G. Thomas (Eds.), *Presenting Saunders Lewis* (pp. 127–141). Cardiff, Wales: University of Wales Press. (Original work published 1962.)
Lewis, S. (1975). *Egwyddorion cenedlaetholdeb: Principles of nationalism*. Cardiff, Wales: Plaid Cymru. (Original work published 1926.)
Lindsay, J. (1974). *A history of the north Wales slate industry*. Newton Abbot, England: David & Charles.
Lloyd, D. M. (1949). *Plaid Cymru and its message*. Cardiff, Wales: Plaid Cymru.
Lloyd, J. E. (1911). *A history of Wales from the earliest times to the Edwardian conquest* (Vols. 1, 2). London: Longmans, Green.
Macauley, T. B. (1913). *The history of England from the accession of James the Second, volume 1*. London: Macmillan. (Original work published 1848.)
Manners, G. (1964). A profile of the new south Wales. In G. Manners (Ed.), *South Wales in the sixties: Studies in industrial geography* (pp. 31–74). New York: Macmillan.
Manners, G., & Minchinton, W. E. (1964). A case for regional planning. In G. Manners (Ed.), *South Wales in the sixties: Studies in industrial geography* (pp. 231–242). New York: Macmillan.
Matthews, E. G. (1971). *Wales and the European Common Market*. Cardiff, Wales: Plaid Cymru.
McNeill, J. T. (1974). *The Celtic churches: A history A.D. 200 to 1200*. Chicago: University of Chicago Press.
Miliband, R. (1982). *Capitalist democracy in Britain*. Oxford, England: Oxford University Press.
Minchinton, W. E. (1964). The evolution of the regional economy. In G. Manners (Ed.), *South Wales in the sixties: Studies in industrial geography* (pp. 1–29). New York: Macmillan.
Minchinton, W. E. (Ed.). (1969). *Industrial south Wales, 1750–1913: Essays in Welsh economic history*. London: Frank Cass.

Morgan, G. (1966). *The dragon's tongue: The fortunes of the Welsh language*. Narberth, Pembrokeshire, Wales: H. G. Walters.
Morgan, K. O. (1963). *Wales in British politics, 1868–1922*. Cardiff, Wales: University of Wales Press.
Morgan, K. O. (1966). The Merthyr of Keir Hardie. In G. Williams (Ed.), *Merthyr politics: The making of a working-class tradition* (pp. 58–81). Cardiff, Wales: University of Wales Press.
Morgan, K. O. (1972). Welsh politics: Cymru Fydd to Crowther. In R. B. Jones (Ed.), *Anatomy of Wales* (pp. 117–144). Peterston-super-Ely, Glamorgan, Wales: Gwerin.
Morgan, K. O. (1982). *Rebirth of a nation: Wales 1880–1980*. Oxford, England: Oxford University Press.
Morgan, P. (1972). The clouds of witnesses: The Welsh historical tradition. In R. B. Jones (Ed.), *Anatomy of Wales* (pp. 17–42). Peterston-super-Ely, Glamorgan, Wales: Gwerin.
Morgan, P. (1983). From a death to a view: The hunt for the Welsh past in the romantic period. In E. Hobsbawm & T. Ranger (Eds.), *The invention of tradition* (pp. 43–100). Cambridge, England: Cambridge University Press.
Mudiad Ysgolion Meithrin Cymraeg (1975–76). *Adroddiad blynyddol* [Annual report]. Cardiff, Wales.
Muir, R. (1927). *A short history of the British Commonwealth, volume 1*. Yonkers-on-Hudson, NY: World Book Company.
Nagel, J. (1984). The ethnic revolution: The emergence of ethnic nationalism in modern states. *Sociology and Social Research, 68*(4), 417–434.
Nairn, T. (1977). *The break-up of Britain: Crisis and neo-nationalism*. London: NLB.
Nielsen, F. (1985). Toward a theory of ethnic solidarity in modern societies. *American Sociological Review, 50*, 133–149.
O'Barr, W. M., & O'Barr, J. F. (Eds.). (1976). *Language and politics*. The Hague: Mouton.
Olorunsola, V. A. (Ed.). (1972). *The politics of cultural sub-nationalism in Africa*. Garden City, NY: Doubleday.
Olson, M. (1971). *The logic of collective action: Public goods and the theory of groups*. Cambridge, MA: Harvard University Press.
Orwig, D. (1987). Penderfyniad y Basgiaid [The Basques' decision]. *Y Faner* (November 6), 10–11.
Osmond, J. (1974). *The centralist enemy*. Llandybie, Dyfed, Wales: Christopher Davies.
Osmond, J. (1977). *Creative conflict: The politics of Welsh devolution*. London: Routledge & Kegan Paul.
Pelling, H. (1965). *The origins of the Labour Party, 1880–1900*. London: Oxford University Press.
Pierce, T. J. (1959). The age of the two Llywelyns. In A. J. Roderick (Ed.), *Wales through the ages, volume 1* (pp. 113–120). Llandybie, Carmarthenshire, Wales: Christopher Davies.
Pi-Sunyer, O. (1980). Dimensions of Catalan nationalism. In C. R. Foster (Ed.), *Nations without a state: Ethnic minorities in western Europe* (pp. 101–115). New York: Praeger.

Plaid Cymru (1943). *TVA for Wales*. Caernarfon, Wales.
Plaid Cymru (1944). *Plan electricity for Wales*. Cardiff, Wales: The London Branch of the Welsh Nationalist Party.
Plaid Cymru (1947). *Mynnwn Gymru rydd* [We demand a free Wales]. Cardiff, Wales.
Plaid Cymru (1950). *Seiliau hanesyddol cenedlaetholdeb Cymru* [The historical bases of Welsh nationalism]. Cardiff, Wales.
Plaid Cymru (1970). *An economic plan for Wales*. Cardiff, Wales.
Plaid Cymru (1976). *Program, Plaid Cymru Annual Conference, 21–24 October 1976*. Cardiff, Wales.
Plaid Cymru (1978). *Program, Plaid Cymru Annual Conference, 19–22 October 1978*. Cardiff, Wales.
Plaid Cymru (1980). *Program, Plaid Cymru Annual Conference, 22–25 October 1980*. Cardiff, Wales.
Plaid Cymru (1981a). *Program, Plaid Cymru Annual Conference, 29 October–1 November 1981*. Cardiff, Wales.
Plaid Cymru (1981b). *Report of the Plaid Cymru Commission of Inquiry*. Cardiff, Wales.
Plaid Cymru (1982). *Program, Plaid Cymru Annual Conference, 28–30 October 1982*. Cardiff, Wales.
Price, M. (1974). *A modern geography of Wales*. Llandybie, Carmarthenshire, Wales: Christopher Davies.
Randall, P. J. (1972). Wales in the structure of central government. *Public Administration Journal* (Autumn), 352–372.
Rees, G. L. (1972). The Welsh economy. In R. B. Jones (Ed.), *Anatomy of Wales* (pp. 55–83). Peterston-super-Ely, Glamorgan, Wales: Gwerin.
Rees, I. B. (1975). *The Welsh political tradition*. Cardiff, Wales: Plaid Cymru. (Original work published 1961.)
Rees, J. F. (1963). *The problem of Wales and other essays*. Cardiff, Wales: University of Wales Press.
Richmond, A. H. (1984). Ethnic nationalism and postindustrialism. *Ethnic and Racial Studies, 7*(1), 4–18.
Roberts, G. (1959a). The significance of 1284. In A. J. Roderick (Ed.), *Wales through the ages, volume 1* (pp. 129–137). Llandybie, Carmarthenshire, Wales: Christopher Davies.
Roberts, G. (1959b). Wales on the eve of the Norman conquest. In A. J. Roderick (Ed.), *Wales through the ages, volume 1* (pp. 74–80). Llandybie, Carmarthenshire, Wales: Christopher Davies.
Roberts, R. O. (1969). Bank of England branch discounting, 1826–59. In W. E. Minchinton (Ed.), *Industrial south Wales, 1750–1914: Essays in Welsh economic history* (pp. 173–189). London: Frank Cass.
Rockett, R. L. (1981). *Ethnic nationalities in the Soviet Union: Sociological perspectives on a historical problem*. New York: Praeger.
Rokkan, S., & Urwin, D. W. (Eds.). (1982). *The politics of territorial identity: Studies in European regionalism*. London: Sage.
Rowlands, E. (1972). The politics of regional administration: The establishment of the Welsh Office. *Public Administration Journal* (Autumn), 333–351.
Rudolph, J. R., Jr., & Thompson, R. J. (1985). Ethnoterritorial movements and

the policy process: Accommodating nationalist demands in the developed world. *Comparative Politics, 17*(3), 291–311.
Sanderson, E. (1893). *History of England and the British Empire: A record of constitutional, naval, military, political and literary events from B.C. 55 to A.D. 1890.* London: Frederick Warne.
Smith, A. D. (1971). *Theories of nationalism.* New York: Harper & Row.
Smith, A. D. (1976). Introduction: The formation of nationalist movements. In A. D. Smith (Ed.), *Nationalist movements* (pp. 1–30). London: Macmillan.
Smith, A. D. (1981). *The ethnic revival.* Cambridge, England: Cambridge University Press.
Smith, D. (1984). *Wales! Wales?* London: George Allen & Unwin.
Thomas, B. (1962). Wales and the Atlantic economy. In B. Thomas (Ed.), *The Welsh economy: Studies in expansion* (pp. 1–29). Cardiff, Wales: The University of Wales Press.
Thomas, B. (1969). The migration of labour into the Glamorganshire coalfield, 1861–1911. In W. E. Minchinton (Ed.), *Industrial south Wales, 1750–1914: Essays in Welsh economic history* (pp. 37–56). London: Frank Cass.
Thomas, C. (1958). Dr. D. J. Davies: A biography. In C. Thomas (Ed.), *Towards Welsh freedom: Twenty-seven articles by Dr. D. J. Davies* (pp. 3–9). Cardiff, Wales: Plaid Cymru.
Tiryakian, E. A., & Rogowski, R. (Eds.). (1985). *New nationalisms of the developed West: Toward explanation.* Boston: Allen & Unwin.
Tiryakian, E. A., & Rogowski, R. (Eds.). (1985). *New nationalisms of the developed West: Toward explanation.* Boston: Allen and Unwin.
Tomkins, C., & Lovering, J. (1973). *Location, size, ownership and control tables for Welsh industry.* Bangor, Wales: Department of Economics, University College of North Wales.
Tout, T. F. (1923). *An advanced history of Great Britain from the earliest times to 1923.* London: Longmans, Green.
Trevelyan, G. M. (1926). *History of England.* London: Longmans, Green.
Undeb Cenedlaethol Athrawon Cymru (1977). *Information relevant to the Association's application for inclusion in the list of trade unions.* Cardiff, Wales.
Urwin, D. W. (1982). Territorial structures and political developments in the United Kingdom. In S. Rokkan & D. W. Urwin (Eds.), *The politics of territorial identity: Studies in European regionalism* (pp. 19–73). London: Sage.
van Amersfoort, H., & van der Wusten, H. (1981). Democratic stability and ethnic parties. *Ethnic and Racial Studies, 4*(4), 476–485.
Verdery, K. (1976). Ethnicity and local systems: The religious organization of Welshness. In C. A. Smith (Ed.), *Regional analysis, volume II: Social systems* (pp. 191–227). New York: Academic Press.
Vickers, K. H. (1914). *England in the later middle ages.* London: Methuen.
Welsh National Water Development Authority (1975). *Fact sheet, Wales: Where rural beauty is an added expense.* Brecon, Powys, Wales.
Whyte, W. F. (1955). *Street corner society* (2nd ed.). Chicago: University of Chicago Press.
Williams, D. (1950). *A history of modern Wales.* London: John Murray.

Williams, D. J. (1973). Saunders Lewis—a man of destiny. In A. R. Jones & G. Thomas (Eds.), *Presenting Saunders Lewis* (pp. 3–5). Cardiff, Wales: University of Wales Press.
Williams, G. (Ed.). (1966). *Merthyr politics: The making of a working-class tradition*. Cardiff, Wales: University of Wales Press.
Williams, G. (1987). *Recovery, reorientation and reformation: Wales c. 1415–1642*. Oxford, England: Clarendon.
Williams, G. A. (1982). Land of our fathers. *Marxism Today* (August), 22–30.
Williams, G. A. (1985). *When was Wales? A history of the Welsh*. Harmondsworth, Middlesex, England: Penguin.
Williams, G. J. (1972). *The vale of Glamorgan: Its history and traditions*. Cardiff, Wales: Plaid Cymru. (Original work published 1953.)
Williams, G. J. (n.d.). *The Welsh tradition of Gwent*. Cardiff, Wales: Plaid Cymru. (Original work published 1958.)
Williams, J. E. C. (1959). Early Welsh literature. In A. J. Roderick (Ed.), *Wales through the ages, volume 1* (pp. 42–49). Llandybie, Carmarthenshire, Wales: Christopher Davies.
Williams, J. L. (1973). The Welsh language in education. In M. Stephens (Ed.), *The Welsh language today* (pp. 92–109). Llandysul, Wales: Gomer.
Williams, J. L. (1976). *The Schools Council and the national language of Wales*. Cardiff, Wales: Schools Council Committee for Wales.
Williams, W. O. (1960). The union of England and Wales. In A. J. Roderick (Ed.), *Wales through the ages, volume 2* (pp. 16–23). Swansea, Wales: Christopher Davies.

Index

Aberdare, 57, 72
Abertillery, 57
Aberystwyth, 46 (*see also* University of Wales, University College Aberystwyth)
Aberystwyth Welsh School, 51–52
Abse, Leo, 57
Acadian nationalism, 110
Act of Union, 8, 10, 28, 35
Agriculture, 64; Ministry of, 88; Welsh Department of, 86, 102
Agriculture Act of 1947, 64
Alsatian nationalist movement, 97
American Black nationalism, 19–20
Anglesey, 76 (*see also* Ynys Môn)
Anglican Church, 11–12
Annan Report, 58

Basques, 1, 97, 112–13
Bebb, W. Ambrose, 29
Bevan, Aneurin, 14
Bilingual road signs, 46, 47
Blue Books Report, 66
Bowen Committee, 47
British Broadcasting Corporation, 55, 102

British Schools Council, Welsh Committee, 54, 56
Brittany, 1, 97
Bureaucracy: British, 16; Welsh, 5–6, 16–17, 53–54, 94, 101–3, 112. *See also* Welsh infrastructure, Welsh organizations.
Bureau of Unrepresented European Nations, 97

Caernarfon, 71, 76; Boroughs, 57
Caerphilly, 73
Capitalism, 59–60, 67–68
Cardiff, 52, 71, 97
Carmarthen, 73, 93, 103
Coal industry, 61–62, 65, 68, 70, 80, 85
Collective action, theory of, 6–7; and political separatism, 7–8
Confederation of British Industry, 17, 84, 88, 90, 98
Conscription, 69

Conservative Party/government, 49, 54, 57, 75, 87, 92, 96, 98, 104
Cornwall, 8–9, 109
Corsican nationalism, 1

Council for Wales, 87
Crawford Report, 58
Cultural division of labor, 4–5, 10, 16, 64 (*see also* Internal colonialism)
Cymdeithas yr Iaith Gymraeg, 45–48, 49, 50, 73, 102, 107; and Plaid Cymru, 47–48, 107
Cymru Fydd, 12–13, 67, 83

Davies, D. J., 67, 68, 80
Davies, Gwilym Prys, 43
Davies, Noëlle, 68
Davies, S. O., 99
Depression, 14, 62, 66
Diffusion-competition model, 5
Disestablishment, 11–12
Distribution of Industries Act, 63
Dyfed, 46, 58

Economic planning, Welsh, 17, 64, 69, 71, 88, 101, 103 (*see also* Regional development programs)
Economy, Welsh, 61–65, 93
Education, 24, 25, 40, 51–53, 57, 66, 88, 102, 107, 109; Welsh Department of, 86, 102
Education Act of 1944, 52, 53, 102
Edwards, Huw T., 87
Edwards, Ifan ab Owen, 52
Edwards, Owen M., 24
Eisteddfod, National, 23–24
Elections: general, 2, 9, 48, 71, 91, 92, 104, 110, 112, 117, 119–21; local government, 104, 113; parliamentary by-, 9, 33, 43, 57, 69, 73, 104, 118
Electricity, 69–70, 81
Ellis, T. E., 35
Emigration, 62–63, 66
English immigration, 53, 111
Ethnic nationalism: Alsatians, 97; American Blacks, 19–20;
Basque, 1, 97, 112–13; Breton, 1, 97; in Britain, 8–10; in Cornwall, 8–9, 109; Corsican, 1; and economic forces, 59–60; and ethnic infrastructure, 110; Francophones in New Brunswickk, 110; Hispanics in U.S., 108; historical background, 2–3; and internal colonialism, 60, 61, 110–11; in the Jura, 1; Native Americans, 20, 108; north of England, 8–9, 109; Quebec, 1, 18, 110; and regional culture, 109; Scottish, 2–3, 8, 91, 110–11; in Soviet Union, 20; in Third World, 108. *See also* Nationalism, Welsh nationalism.
European Economic Community, 84, 97–98, 112, 113
European Parliament, 98, 99, 113
Evans, Gwynfor, 30–31, 35, 48, 49, 73, 93

Fascism, 69
Fires: in Lleyn, 42–43; second-home, 48
Flint, 52, 58, 80
Free-rider dilemma, 6–7
Free Wales Army, 48

Gas industry, 70
General Strike, 67
George, David Lloyd, *see* Lloyd George, David
Griffiths, James, 87
Gruffydd, Moses, 57
Gwilym, Eurfyl ap, 73
Gwynedd, 58, 113; County Council, 49

Hardie, Keir, 14
Hispanics in U.S., 108
Housing, 75–76, 111; second homes, 48, 58
Hughes Parry Committee, 46
Humphreys, Emyr, 35
Hydro Group, 78

Independent Labour Party, 14, 80
Industrial democracy, 76–77
Industrial Investment Act, 63
Industrial Revolution, 3, 61
Internal colonialism, 4–5, 60–61, 79–80, 110 (*see also* Cultural divisions of labor)
Iron industry, 61, 64–65

Index

Isaac, Norah, 52
Iwan, Dafydd, 78
Iwan, Emrys ap, *see* Jones, Robert Ambrose

Jenkins, John, 58
Jones, Fred, 57
Jones, Geraint, 57
Jones, H. R., 57
Jones, Ieuan Wyn, 112
Jones, Michael D., 35
Jones, Robert Ambrose (Emrys ap Iwan), 35
Jura, 1

Kilbrandon Commission, 91
Kinnock, Neil, 93

Labor movement, 14
Labour Party/government, 14, 54, 57, 69, 72, 73, 75, 76, 79, 83, 86, 87, 90, 102, 104; and Welsh devolution, 91–93, 94, 99
Lewis, Saunders, 29–30, 41–43, 45, 57, 67–68, 107
Liberal Party, 10, 12–13, 57, 71, 83
Liberation Society, 11
Llafur, 29
Lloyd George, David, 12–13, 35
Lloyd, J. E., 22, 28
Local Employment Act of 1960, 63
London Welsh, 12, 15, 16, 23

Merioneth, 44, 77
Merthyr Tydfil, 61, 62, 76, 77, 99, 113
Mid Glamorgan, 33, 58, 113
Milk Marketing Scheme, 64
Mineworkers, 67; National Union of, 85–86, 89
Modernization: polity, 12, 14–15, 16; state, 4, 14–15, 16, 18; theory, 4
Monmouth, 10, 35
Morgan, Gwyn, 98
Morgannwg, Iolo, *see* Williams, Edward
Mudiad Amddiffyn Cymru, 48
Mudiad Ysgolion Meithrin, 53

Nationalism: ideology of, 3–4, 20; and intrusive bureaucracies, 20, 108; and language, 37–39, 109, 110; and national history, 21–22, 109; and socialism, 14, 110–11; and Welsh infrastructure, 75, 98, 108. *See also* Ethnic nationalism, Welsh nationalism.
National Union of Mineworkers (NUM), *see* Mineworkers, National Union of
Native Americans, 20, 108
Neath, 57
Nonconformity, 11–12, 13, 15
North of England, 8–9, 109
No-to-the-Assembly Campaign, 92, 94

Ogmore, 57

Parliament for Wales Campaign, 71–72, 87
Plaid Cymru: and Cymdeithas yr Iaith, 47–48; and economic planning, 69–70, 71, 74–75, 103–5, 106, 112; economic policy, 67–69, 73–74; and the EEC, 97; in general elections, 9, 71, 117, 119–21; and housing, 75–76; Hydro Group, 78; and industrial democracy, 76; internal development, 72–73, 81, 93, 103–4, 105–6; in local government, 9, 104, 113; National Left, 78; in parliamentary by-elections, 9, 33, 43, 57, 69, 73, 118; party history, 9, 57, 81; and the referendum for a Welsh Assembly, 92, 93–94; Research Group, 73; and second-home fires, 48–49; and socialism, 72, 74, 75–79, 81, 82, 110–11; Special Commission on the Future of the Party, 50–51, 77, 79; and S4C, 49–50; and Wales TUC, 70, 88–89, 90; and Welsh Assembly proposals, 93–94, 99; and Welsh history, 29–34; and the Welsh language, 40, 41, 43–45, 49–51, 107, 108; and Welsh water, 96–97

Pontypool, 57

Quebec, 1, 18, 110

Reactive ethnicity model, 5 (*see also* Cultural division of labor, Internal colonialism)
Referendum: EEC membership, 90; in Quebec, 18; for a Scottish Assembly, 18, 91–92; for a Welsh Assembly, 18, 57, 91–93. *See also* Welsh Assembly, Welsh devolution.
Regional development programs, 17, 60, 66, 71, 75, 79–80, 101, 103–4
Regional Employment Premium, 63, 104
Research Group, *see* Plaid Cymru Research Group
Revolutionary Communist Party, 57
Rhondda, 52, 62, 67, 73
Rhymney, 113
Roberts, Emrys, 48

Scotland, 1–2, 5, 8, 91–92, 109–10
Scottish Nationalist Party, 9–10, 110–11
Secretary of State for Wales, *see* Welsh Office
Sianel Pedwar Cymru (S4C), 49–50, 55, 98, 102, 105
Socialism: decentralist, 78–79, 82; and nationalism, 14, 66, 80, 110; in Plaid Cymru, 72, 74, 75–80, 110–11

Third World, 60; nationalism, 108
Thomas, D. A., 13
Thomas, Dafydd Elis, 44, 49, 77, 78–79
Transport and General Workers Union, 89

Undeb Cenedlaethol Athrawon Cymru, 54
Unemployment, 62, 63, 65
United Nations, 57
University of Wales, 13, 22, 105; University College, Aberystwyth, 22, 35, 46; University College, Bangor, 22, 35; University College, Cardiff, 35

Urdd Gobaith Cymru, 52

Valentine, Lewis, 57

Wales-for-the-Assembly Campaign, 92, 93
Wales Gas Board, 70
Wales: The Way Ahead, 64
Wales Trades Union Council, 17, 70, 84, 88–90, 92, 94, 98, 112
Water: Act of 1973, 95; Charges Equalisation Bill, 95; and nationalism, 94–95; Welsh rates, 50, 95–96
Welfare state, 63, 66, 84, 85–86; and political nationalism, 17, 18, 84, 98, 101–2; and the Welsh bureaucracy, 16, 80, 84, 98
Welsh Assembly, 18, 57, 84, 91–94, 112; compared to Scottish Assembly, 91; and Wales TUC support, 90
Welsh Courts Act, 46
Welsh Department of Education, 54
Welsh Development Agency, 17, 64
Welsh devolution, 88, 94, 102, 103 (*see also* Welsh Assembly)
Welsh history: and British history, 25–29; nineteenth-century interpretation, 15, 22; and political nationalism, 24–25, 29–35, 105; twentieth-century interpretations, 15, 22–23, 29
Welsh infrastructure, 5–6, 10, 17, 53–57, 75, 80, 86, 88, 97, 98, 102 (*see also* Bureaucracy, Welsh organizations)
Welsh Intermediate Education Act, 12
Welsh Joint Education Committee, 53, 54, 55, 102
Welsh language: background, 10, 37–39; in education, 39, 40, 102, 111–12; and internal colonialism, 66–67; in the National Eisteddfod, 23–24; in nineteenth-century nationalism, 15, 39, 51, 56; and political nationalism, 41–45, 102, 105, 107; status, 40, 46–47, 111; in twentieth-century nationalism,

15–16, 39–41, 56–57, 107–8; and the Welsh bureaucracy, 41, 51, 101–2
Welsh Language Act of 1967, 40, 46
Welsh Language Education Development Committee, 56, 102
Welsh nationalism: and the British state, 83–84; and internal colonialism, 65–66, 79–80, 104; and national history, 29–30, 34, 105; nineteenth-century, 10–14, 15; and socialism, 66; and the Wales TUC, 89–90; and the Welsh language, 37–41, 50–51, 102, 107–9, 111–12; and Welsh water, 94–95. *See also* Ethnic nationalism, Nationalism, Plaid Cymru.
Welsh Nationalist Party, 14, 57, 67–69, 83, 105–6; economic policy, 16, 65–66, 67–68; and Welsh history, 29–30, 105; and the Welsh language, 40, 41–43. *See also* Plaid Cymru.
Welsh Nursery Schools Movement, *see* Mudiad Ysgolion Meithrin
Welsh Office, 17, 49, 53, 54, 55, 64, 84, 86–88, 97, 98, 102, 103, 104, 111, 112
Welsh organizations, 35, 55–56; bureaucratic, 17, 53–54; nineteenth-century, 13, 51; nongovernmental, 17, 54. *See also* Bureaucracy, Welsh infrastructure.
Welsh Republican Movement, 43, 71
Welsh schools movement, 52–53, 102, 107–8, 111 (*see also* Education)
Welsh Socialist Republican Movement, 78
Welsh Sunday Closing Act, 12
Welsh Water Authority, 84, 94–97
Wigley, Dafydd, 76, 77
Williams, D. E., 57
Williams, Edward (Iolo Morgannwg), 23
Williams, G. J., 29, 35
Williams, Phil, 51, 73, 79, 81, 88
World War II, 63, 69
Working-class history, 29
Wright, George, 89, 90

Ynys Môn, 112 (*see also* Anglesey)

About the Author

CHARLOTTE AULL DAVIES was born in Lexington, Kentucky in 1942. She received B.S. and M.S. degrees in Mathematics. Subsequently she studied Cultural Anthropology and, in 1978, received the Ph.D. degree from Duke University in that field with emphasis on complex societies. The subject of her dissertation was Ethnic Nationalism in Wales. In 1978–79 she studied at the University of Wales, Swansea on a postdoctoral research fellowship from the Social Sciences Research Council. She was continually resident in Wales until 1985, when she returned to the United States as Visiting Assistant Professor in the College of Criminal Justice, University of South Carolina. She is married, her husband is Welsh, and they have one daughter.